DEATH'S SUMMER COAT

DEATH'S SUMMER COAT

What the History of Death and Dying
Can Tell Us about Life and Living

B R A N D Y S C H I L L A C E

PEGASUS BOOKS
NEW YORK LONDON

Death's Summer Coat

Pegasus Books LLC
80 Broad Street, 5th Floor
New York, NY 10004

ISBN: 978-1-60598-938-9

10 9 8 7 6 5 4 3 2 1

Printed in the United States of America
Distributed by W. W. Norton & Company, Inc.

CONTENTS

⟡

Introduction

MEET THE NEW (OLD) DEATH

Why a book like this
one, and why now?

The theatre was box-like, crouched behind razor wire off the strip in Los Angeles. Unremarkable, really; a dust-coloured square barely discernible from the others that dotted Beverly Boulevard under a hot October sun. You weren't going to miss it, though. There were too many people out front, and nearly everyone – whether in evening attire or metal studs – wore black. A funeral? No, though the Grim Reaper was in attendance (with an actual scythe). A concert? An art show? Not quite. Here, not far from Hollywood, were gathered scholars, morticians, curators and an interested public for the first 'death cabaret' – part of the first ever Death Salon. The talks and events showcased something most people rarely, if ever, consider: our own mortality.

We die. We know this, in principle, and yet in the Western world we don't live with the idea of death. We refrain from thinking about it, we avoid reflecting upon it, and death is something most of us simply don't talk about. Death Salon is an unusual organisation in that it chooses death as a focus for discussion, but it's part of an emerging 'death-positive' movement, one that includes death cafes and death dinners. These gatherings call for the breaking of taboos, a desire to reclaim ground that has been lost – particularly in the West – during a century and a half of sanitisation and silence. Insulated by their relative wealth, health systems and the successes of hygiene and sterilisation, post-industrial nations have the privilege of a protective screen from unmediated images of death. Even so, these advances cannot ultimately protect us from death itself. It's time to rejoin the conversation.

Jon Underwood, a former British council worker, founded Death Cafe in 2011, inspired by the ideas of Bernard Crettaz, a Swiss sociologist who began a decade ago to encourage people to talk freely about death. Tea, cake and death are the order of the day, and many new death cafes (not run by Underwood) have sprouted up here and there as places to speak about the inevitable. These mortality meetings tend to create a stir, showing up in blog feeds, on Twitter and Facebook, and in news sites such as the *Huffington Post* and the *New York Times*. Even more recently, Kate Granger, a thirty-one-year-old British physician with terminal cancer, has committed to live-tweeting her final moments, and comedian Laurie Kilmartin (a writer for the Conan O'Brien show) live-tweeted her father's last days in hospice care. But these attempts at making death part of the conversation are not without their problems – and detractors. Some commentators question whether making public these personal events is an appropriate use of social media, while others worry that these are novelty encounters which will ultimately lead to a clichéd sense of death rather than true engagement with it. Regardless of what side you take, these platforms suggest an increasing number of us want to explore death – or, at the very least, to broach the subject.

Why, someone asked recently, are events like Death Salon happening in Europe and the US? Why not elsewhere? To begin with, they *are* happening elsewhere; death cafes have been held in Hong Kong and in India. In an article entitled 'Care to Talk About Death Over Coffee?' the *Times of India* asked people what they thought of the concept. One respondent, Soma Mukherjee, replied: 'I don't know if it will really work here [because] death is discussed from the time the first pet or grand-uncle dies.' In cultures where death already has a place, where it already appears as a normal and approachable subject, there need be no taboo-breaking. It's only where we have lost the ability to discuss these subjects openly that we need new perspective.

Of course, in some ways, we are talking. The overwhelming popularity of Mary Roach's humorous look at what happens after death, *Stiff: The Curious Lives of Human Cadavers*, is a good example. Roach proves that we can learn a lot by studying the hidden, or at least less familiar, practices of the body after death – from bodysnatching to 'medical' cannibalism. The dead body, the cadaver, may reveal a lot about anatomy and the functions of the body. The history of those bodies can tell us a great deal about how perspectives have changed. But death in the abstract is a very different thing from death closer to home; it touches our families, our homes, our hearts. Death is a balancing act: we know it will happen to us, to those we love, and yet we live in denial. That denial often leaves us entirely unprepared for the other element of death: grief.

Most of us remember 'the sex talk'. I got mine early, after catching the neighbours at it. I was five, and met my mother at the door when she got home, demanding to know 'how it was done'. (I was horrified by the explanation, as most of us probably were.) It has long served as a kind of cultural touch-stone in Western society: frequently referred to as 'the birds and the bees' or, more ominously, 'the talk'. But how many of us recall any similar kind of conversation on the subject of death? Or grief? Hospice care provides one means of readying the dying and their families, but more often the mortally sick go to a hospital, where they remain until death. Their bodies are transported from that sterile room to a funeral home, where they are prepared without our knowledge and often without our input. It's little wonder that discussion of death is taboo. My best friend's mother, a breast cancer patient, tried repeatedly to talk about the looming possibility of her own death, only to be told that she should not speak of it. It is a strange irony: the last thing we are supposed (or allowed) to do when preparing to meet death is talk about death. Can you imagine the inverse? We would not plan for the birth of a child without addressing the subject of labour. Major events demand adequate preparation — more than that, they require solemnity, significance. These make up our cultural rituals, and rituals have enormous power.

We find ourselves today in a culture of opposites: bent on living forever, but committed to the disposable nature of absolutely everything else. Looking to find meaning isn't an arbitrary quest: it is the human condition, and rituals are human events that help us find that meaning. While the word itself suggests imagery from religious practice, ritual really refers to behaviour — actions performed with intention and significance. They may be as simple as a handshake or as complex as a rite of passage, but they stand for so much more. Rituals are the fabric of our cultural identities and they enable us to proceed through life's great moments.

Has something happened to our rituals for death? For dying

and for grieving? The silence that currently surrounds mortality is actually comparatively recent. In the death announcements of eighteenth-century Britain and the US, people did not 'pass on'; they died. Euphemisms were used, too, but not often. Someone might, on occasion, 'kick the bucket' (an expression that probably refers to the process of slaughtering hogs) – and in the case of hanged criminals, they might 'swing home'. But the real push towards euphemisms for death happened later, mainly in the mid to late nineteenth century. This shift can be seen even in the American funeral announcements shown here, which changed the wording in death notices from 'moulders

Death notice from the nineteenth century.

Death notice from the twentieth century.

here' to 'slumbers here' in the space of a decade. References to decay are removed for the more esoteric image of sleep; but why? What changed in Western culture? Fast-forward to the twenty-first century, and our language is even less able to confront the reality of death. We avoid using the word itself, talk in metaphors about 'brave battles' and shy away from anything that might remind us of our own mortality. What drove us to sanitise death, and in so doing, make it foreign and unfamiliar?

Eternal or disposable?

Our medical establishment is primarily concerned with prolonging life, not with preparing us for death. Death has become the enemy of medicine, to be fought at all costs, regardless of the situation. This is evident from the various debates about assisted suicide and enforced life support, and legal cases such as that of Terri Schiavo, a woman in a vegetative state whose feeding tube was removed only after seven years, fourteen appeals, five suits in federal district court and a Supreme Court decision. Major companies are investing in ways to prevent the ageing process – Google recently got in on the act with Calico, its biotech subsidiary aiming to 'cure death'. Ray Kurzweil, an engineer, philosopher and inventor described by *Forbes* as 'the ultimate thinking machine', suggests that advances in nanotechnology will allow humans to live forever. While this sounds far-fetched, it is essentially the ultimate mission of Western medical and scientific research: replacement parts, better genes and the end of all diseases. We have not moved towards the acceptance of death, but rather the erasure of it.

But, as my grandmother was fond of saying, everything dies. Though separated by culture, context and chronicity, all humans must face the coming of death in a way distinct from our nearest mammal cousins. When we witness death, we must grapple with its finality, but also with our own mortality and the knowledge that one day we too will die. Whereas once this was understood as the natural order of things, we now find ourselves conflicted and less willing to see death as 'natural'. If anything, death breaks into our lives as an unexpected surprise.

Our disavowal of death's naturalness makes it harder to grieve properly. The Victorians had incredibly complex mourning rituals, including mourning jewellery, photographs of the recently dead (memento mori photography) and the public wearing of mourning clothing. Like birth, death was a social event that drew communities together. In a large city, scarcely a day would go by without some sign of bereavement being visible. Compare this with today, when illness and death are either hidden away in hospitals or sensationalised through popular culture, and when prolonged grief is likely to be medicated as abnormal rather than openly acknowledged as an inevitable part of life. Elisabeth Kübler-Ross, a Swiss-American psychiatrist, developed her theory of the five stages of grief in 1969 as a response to the lack of information on death and dying in the curriculum of medical schools – but even these stages hardly cover the enormous range of emotions that accompany death, and they certainly weren't a plan for how to go about the process of grieving.

Religious service and practice once provided a universal framework for dealing with and understanding death; they still do, of course, but for many people today, these traditions don't reflect their beliefs and experience, and little has replaced them. In a 2011 article for *Prospect* magazine ('Death Becomes Us'), Sarah Murray addresses the plight of her atheist father; he believed fervently that humans were but organic matter, but nonetheless wanted his ashes to be spread in a churchyard. His desire was not a return to belief, but rather, as the author writes, recognition that 'dismissing the significance of "organic matter" is not that easy'. We long for a permanence of 'things' and places to grieve. This is just as true in the wake of great tragedies such as the 2005 London bombings, the downing of Malaysian Airlines Flight M-17 or the collapse of the Twin Towers. Our need to grieve can become explosive if kept inside us. It needs an outlet. Otherwise, where are we to put all that sadness? Or – to put it another way – what are we to do with ourselves?

In the relentless rush and hurry of modern life, too often death comes like an unplanned interruption. But the world keeps moving on, swift in its course, and often the experience of death whips past us in a series of distorted scenes we hardly recall and decisions we scarcely remember making. This is especially true if death comes suddenly, or if the dead person made no explicit plans for their passing. However, when my grandfather died, things happened slowly enough for me to take some notice. My cousin officiated the ceremony – the funeral parlour was a quiet house not far from the family cemetery. We had coffee upstairs in the faux-brick kitchen, and I had time to think about death as something – almost a someone – to be approached intimately. To me, this was new. But it isn't new. It is old – nearly as old as history. Rather than continuing to avoid death, or to fear it, what if we changed our perception? Might we conceive of death, instead, as the winding down of life's frantic clock – and dying as a means of coming to terms with our identities, our loved ones, ourselves?

We do still have rituals. Why aren't they helping? It is hard to examine something when you are too near to see it properly, and without engagement, reflection and sometimes reinvention, rituals can lose their meaning. It is often easier to understand one's own country by looking outward. The mediation of distance is important, not because it prevents us from facing death, but because it is only from a distance that we can appreciate the vast complexity surrounding it. We'll start by looking at certain grief rituals and death practices of cultures different from the West, from sky burial to mummification, and then consider how they compare with the history of the Western approach to death and dying. If knowledge is power, then greater knowledge about how death is viewed elsewhere and in times gone past is a powerful tool to help us think about whether we can do better in the here and now. Looking for ways of approaching our mortality isn't foolish – it is a war on fear and misinformation, and on that vacuum of silence.

Death's summer coat

For many centuries, death was an expected part of life, but in the past 150 years, our approach to death in the West has changed markedly. For the most part, we aren't aware of this change – but if we don't know where we've come from, we aren't likely to know where we're heading. Through the help of 'weird' science, history, literature and a number of previously unpublished photos, this book reimagines the journey the West has taken – and takes a closer look at our final destination. Once we meet death and keep it near, it ceases to threaten us, ceases to be alien. Death, when embraced, can be the means to healing and to progressing through grief for the living. It can also be our greatest means of connection. The chapters that follow are about 'putting on' rituals, wearing them as the vestal garments often used in ceremony. Wrapped up in these, in death's 'summer coat', we find it easier to approach our common end.

As a medical-humanities scholar, I have lived my professional life at the intersection of several fields: history, literature, medicine, anthropology. Intersections are valuable. The inroad that another person's belief makes as it comes into contact with my own is not an invasion so much as an invitation. Sharing our stories provides hope and community, so that none of us needs to face death alone in the silent dark. Learning about other practices is enticing partly because the unfamiliar looks so new; that unfamiliarity encourages us to engage with every aspect, to ask questions, to wonder and to reconsider our own ways of doing things in turn. We do not need to agree with a cultural tradition or religious belief in order to acknowledge its value and its power.

The title of this book is not intended to put a rosy hue on what is hard and unfathomable. It is not an attempt to make palatable a bitter pill. To me, the phrase 'death's summer coat' is recognition that all things ephemeral are made lovely in their brevity. We long for spring or summer despite – or perhaps because of – the seasons being fleeting: a glimpse of life's bud, followed by autumn and the long, dark winter. We ritualise the coming of the warmer months by cleaning our houses, planning reading lists and summer holidays, celebrating Easter or any of the other holidays that rejoice in the thaw. We shed our layers and put on new clothes like a new skin. Death's summer coat is life's unexpected beauty, and when each of us passes ultimately into that last winter, I believe it, too, will be followed by a new spring. What that spring will be like, I don't know. Many religions describe it. Many who are not religious nonetheless see continuity in our return to the earth, and our part in the life cycle and the seasons.

It's time to meet the new (old) death.

Chapter 1

DEAD AND KNOWING IT

What to expect when
you're expecting death

'**A**wake,' my mother said. 'To sit with the dead.'

We were on our way to West Virginia, to an unremarkable two-storey colonial where my grandfather's remains had been washed and laid out for viewing. It had been raining all night, but apparently no one in this homey funeral parlour had been sleeping. They'd been sitting up with the body. Sitting up – with the body – all night.

There are no good adjectives to describe my initial feelings about this. I was seventeen and grieving, but as I thought about it I realised I wasn't horrified. Shocked, yes, but the idea was strangely enticing, even fascinating. *Really? We do that?* This wasn't my first funeral, but it was the first time I'd encountered the intimacy of a ritual like this one. My West Virginian relatives had traditions I had not encountered before, traditions that still exist around the country even if only in pockets or among particular denominations. The wake struck me with its unfamiliarity, and helped me to look at the buzzing activity that surrounds the newly dead in new ways. I asked myself what seemed like suddenly obvious questions – why wash a body before putting it in the dirt? Why sit awake with someone now permanently asleep? Even the practice of embalming the body (which *prevents* decay) before interring it in the ground (where it is *supposed* to decay) struck me as a very strange thing to do. With only a minor leap of morbid imagination, care of the newly dead began to resemble care of the newly born. And sharing this, I knew, was going to upset people.

Death and birth are not, strictly speaking, as divergent as you might expect. In my work for the Dittrick Medical History Center in Cleveland, Ohio, I curate exhibits on the history of childbirth and midwifery. *The Kahun Gynaecological Papyrus* was found at El-Lahun, Egypt (Faiyum, Kahun, كاهون) by Flinders Petrie in 1889. It is one of the oldest surviving medical texts and concerns aspects of pregnancy and birth, as well as various associated diseases, around 1800 BC. A woman was rarely so near death as when giving birth, and this is true in Ancient Greece and Rome as well. Expectant mothers would offer miniature statues showing a healthy and safe delivery to a Greek deity such as Asklepios in hopes of protection (or as thanks). As time progressed, more books with better instruction for saving infants appeared, but numerous diseases, poor health and no concept of germ theory meant that mothers and infants still perished together, joining the end of life with its beginning. In fact, death might almost be responsible for the future saving of lives.

Two doctors were busily working to understand pregnant women's bodies in the eighteenth century. William Hunter published *Anatomy of the Human Gravid Uterus* and William Smellie *A Set of Anatomical Tables*. These incredibly lifelike images (by artist Jan van Rymsdyk) helped to explain why things went wrong and how to address problems before they became deadly. The mothers and children pictured here helped obstetrical medicine save countless others, but even so, a woman's child-bearing years were also potentially her *dying years*.

Childbirth and death remain linked today, despite Western scientific advances, but in certain other cultures, reproductive

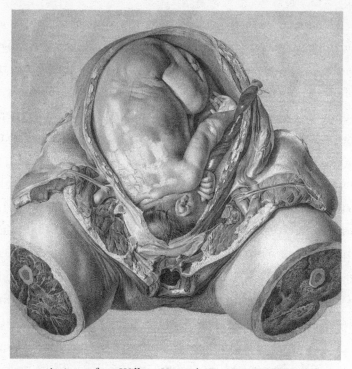

An image from William Hunter's *Gravid Uterus* (1774).

destiny *supersedes* death. If a child died before marrying among the Karo Batak of Sumatra, they were ritually married so that they might, at least symbolically, start a family. In some cultures, 'ghost marriages' are performed for single children who have died; sometimes they are married to the living, and other times to the dead. Similarly, death and rebirth link the community to those who have passed on, from the mythology of the Ancient Greeks to Hindu reincarnation. The idea of 'transmigration' was very important, because the life you led could determine how and when you were reborn in the future . . . or where you would be travelling after death. In his groundbreaking work from 1907, *Death and the Right Hand*, anthropologist Robert Hertz explains funerary rites as consisting of 'two complementary notions': death as a lasting procedure and death as transition. From Egypt to Borneo to Madagascar to India, death was – and sometimes still is – seen primarily as a transitional state, a state of becoming as much as ending. In this nexus of death, birth and rebirth, is death an event or a process? And how does our perspective influence the way we prepare for it?

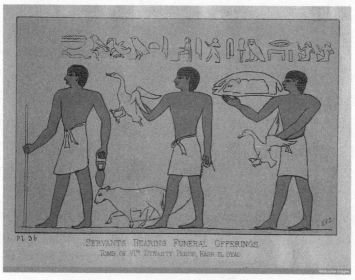

Preparations for the death journey.

Death as event and process

Most of us, whether consciously or not, seek to collect and categorise information. In February 2009, a team led by psychologist Alfonso Caramazza of Harvard University examined brain response and found, rather surprisingly, that the organisation of categories remained the same whether you were sighted or born blind. If you think first of a dog, and then of a hammer, two different category areas of your brain will be active. So far, so good. But if you have never seen a hammer or a dog before in your life, the result will remain exactly the same. How can that be? Apparently, the connections between different areas of our visual cortex and the rest of the brain are almost hardwired. We are born with them; they don't form gradually as we age. That means we are living categorising engines, and this kind of thinking is very useful to us as a species because it allows for quick identification. Bear? Wolf? Lion? All filed under 'animals with teeth, best to avoid'. Rock? Stick? Steel? All under 'potential weapons to thwart animals with teeth'. There is, however, a drawback to this kind of thinking.

We operate with an understanding that one thing is not another; an apple is not an orange, I am not you. But reality is much more complicated. Physics tells us this: the desk I am writing at, in addition to being a hard, sturdy surface, is also a jiggling mass of atoms, a cloud of whizzing electrons and a whole lot of empty space. I know both sets of things are true, but my category-loving brain has enormous difficulty thinking both at once. The same is true of our reaction to death and dying. Death is rarely if ever simply a *thing* – for example, only or merely the event of ceasing to physically live and breathe. It is always *things* – emotions, states of being, a constant flux of changing relations; a closed door that separates one consciousness from another, felt by both the dying and the grieving. In other words, death is *both* an event *and* a process.

Even as I write this, I feel my own need to differentiate: surely death is the event and dying the process? Perhaps. But every day that we live, we also die. Our cells – the skin on our hands, the lining of our internal organs, our blood and other tissues – shed themselves daily and we carry some of this small death about with us. In fact, our houses are filled with the remnants of who we were last week or last year; we are the dust that twinkles in a sunlit swirl from an open window. It is almost easier for me to imagine my own body as that vortex of atoms, with its ever-renewing and decaying pulse. But if I am living, how can I also be dying?

That seeming contradiction represents one of the great human dilemmas. We know we will one day die, and yet we live. Animals know death when they see it; they even express grief or go looking for their deceased litter-mates, housemates or masters when they are gone. However, animals largely recognise the *event* of death rather than the *process* of expecting death. Sociologist Allan Kellehear gives an example about a mare who witnessed her colt being lost to a swollen river. The mother horse ran back and forth along the bank, frantically whinnying. She had witnessed it being buried, but she never expressed any interest in the grave, only in the river. Death happens in a moment, and it's the river she fears, not mortality itself.

That doesn't mean that animals don't grieve. We have many examples of it – too many to ignore. Elephants, for instance, will return to the bones of those that died, sometimes stroking or carrying them about. There are examples from primates as well, and Kellehear even cites stories about animals that feign

Pictorial gravestone, Scotland.

death (like the opossum) to suggest that animals do know what death is, what it looks like and can even imitate it. The difference between the animal kingdom and the human race lies primarily in this: in seeing the death of another, we recognise our own mortality: 'dying' says Kellehear, is 'a self-conscious anticipation of impending death'. We see the herald of our own death, we hear the approaching footsteps and we know that one day, death will come for us. We needn't know the deceased well – it need not even be a human death. All the same, mortality speaks to us.

When I was four years old, I lived with my mother and

grandparents in a white house with two porches. I remember a day in spring, when little bluebells were blooming next to the front steps, I began thinking of each little bell as the life of a person. How long would it live? Fifty years? Maybe I even guessed a hundred. But the point is this: I worried about what would happen when the bluebell's life was all used up. What happened then? The real question, of course, was *what happens when you die?* In my confused ideas about bluebells, I had grasped that no matter what, no living thing would stay the *same*. Change happened. Nothing was permanent. Not even the people I loved. Not even me. Process meant change, and change meant dying.

At what point does dying become death? The knowledge 'I will die' becomes 'I am dying' largely based on timing: when we've been diagnosed with a disease that has no cure, when we are grievously injured, when our own systems begin to go offline. 'Here the "philosophical" point ends,' says Kellehear, 'and the "real" or "short personal countdown" to death begins.' I recall a friend's experience with his father. He asked the doctors when he would get better, when he would experience the return to normal we've all come to expect from our encounters with illness. But this time, there would be no recovery. Suddenly the man's entire world and all of his preparations contracted and needed to be realigned (and in a doctor's office, which is often not the best place for reflection). A mad rush of activity usually follows such a shift in perception, either on the part of the dying or on the part of their loved ones. Last days of care must be considered, funerals planned for, loved ones looked after, the great long-term plans laid aside – and once again, the focus tends to be on the activity and less on the process that the body itself is going through. There are worlds between the healthy human's 'I am dying' and the raw nerves expressed in 'I am dying *now*.' The process and the event overlap as all other ideas collapse around us.

For some of us, understanding how we will die shapes the way that we decide to approach it. My grandfather, whose wake I mentioned earlier, died of lung cancer. At seventy-two, he decided against treatment, asking the doctors merely to make him comfortable for as long as possible. The length of time between his diagnosis and his death was roughly a year. In that time, he was able to set many things in order, not just those things on the checklist of finance, social propriety, family engagement and funeral arrangement, but other, deeper things. As those who would be left behind, we also had time to prepare and then months to watch the deterioration that signalled the end. He died at home under hospice care, in his own bed. The 'event' of his death began as a year-long 'process' before the last beat of his heart, and that period of dying was also a death, or a series of small deaths (some of which we, as his children and grandchildren, also experienced).

Death unexpected

What happens, though, when death cannot be prepared for, or when there isn't time for this sort of process? A few years ago I was seated at a diner with my spouse, preparing to order a late Saturday breakfast. Suddenly, a gentleman in the booth across from us gripped at his throat, half stood and then collapsed on the floor. The scene was confused; people were shouting for 911 and asking if anyone knew CPR. Having once trained as a lifeguard, I joined a waitress in attempting to resuscitate him – he was not choking; he was having a heart attack. It's a fearful thing to have your training tested like that, though I was mainly keeping his pulse and counting for chest compression as the waitress administered breaths. My fingers circled his wrist, and then, after ten minutes, I felt a change that I will never forget. He died, and I felt him go, felt the life slide away beneath the pressure of my fingertips. The paramedics arrived but could not save him. We discovered later that he had an undiagnosed congenital defect and that his heart had burst.

I still recall that moment with peculiar clarity; if ever death was an event rather than a process, surely this was it. I had been present for the moment of separation. But even here, the line is not as clear as you might suppose. How many of us have lived through a minute that felt like hours? Time loses its relevance under the pressure of immeasurable events – it simply does not matter how *long*. A car accident might seem to move in slow motion, slow enough for you to see your life flash before you and to think, suddenly, of those who matter most. In those few cases where people have apparently died and been brought back, they report feeling and seeing everything around them with clarity as well. Whether it is adrenaline, or merely the conscious sense of the impending, under pressure there is often time enough for the smallest of details. More problematic is the concept of brain death, when no activity is detected. Neurologists still struggle with the line that demarcates alive and dead, here and truly gone, something I'll return to in Chapter Six. Ultimately the answer to the question 'where is the line between dying and death' – or between process and event – is this: there probably isn't one. But that should be a comfort to us; there is no wrong way to see it, and that means no wrong way to feel it, either.

I have suggested that expecting one's own death is part of what makes us human, though exactly when in our pre-history we began to understand our mortality is hotly debated. Some argue intentional burials happened as early as 30,000 years ago – and some estimates (particularly those of the archaeologist Francesco d'Errico) say 170,000 years ago. The hunter-gatherer life was difficult, fraught with danger and likely to end suddenly; there were few examples of lingering illness, few chances to accept death slowly or to adjust expectations. Instead, death was ever-present. Every day, the hunter – like the warrior – had to acknowledge that it might be his last. Every member of the community 'took part' in mortality through the deaths of other people. Their elaborate grave rituals, some of which lasted for a year or more, were the inverse of the process my grandfather went through. Instead of the dying making preparations in the twelve months leading up to death, preparations (this time for the other-worldly journey rather than for the death) happened among the *living* in the year that *followed*. Fast-forward to 1913, when Sir James George Frazer documented Fijian after-death rituals; for them, the real work began after death, where the soul would encounter numerous dangers that could, in fact, 'kill' it (really this time). For Fijians, the dying process happened after burial, not before.

Sometimes the deceased soul might linger for months, might even need to be cared for (or feared) by its nearest relations. Among the Arunta, Frazer describes a second ceremony to force a lazy soul on its journey. For these peoples, the burden of 'dying' is carried by the living – a sentiment that anyone who has recently experienced the death of a beloved friend or relative may understand only too well.

Admittedly, among the young and the healthy, facing mortality is generally a distant and somewhat vague proposition. In the developed world, fewer people under the age of thirty have to address the looming unknown. What does it mean to stand upon the precipice of consciousness and look into the void, wondering if we will still know ourselves on the other side (or if there *is* an 'other side')? This is one of the chief complaints against 'death-positive' networks like Death Salon or the death cafes appearing in the US and Europe: those seeking to break death taboos are frequently (though not exclusively) young and able-bodied. How can they really know what death means? The question is slightly wrong-headed, as biological age is no guarantee of insight, but I think there is something else at its heart. In a culture where we are rarely taught to expect death, much less discuss it, it is frequently the aged and the ill who have the most immediate experience of it. To those in terminal pain, who are looking at death in all its faceless ambiguity, it seems perverse that anyone else would try to, and perhaps wrong that they *should* presume to do so. That moment is so personal, so intimate, so crushing, so full of mixed hopes and despair, it is little wonder most people want to avoid thinking or talking about it. But let us consider again – dying is a process carried out by the living. It is, in fact, the most challenging and daunting experience of *life*.

***

I have talked about the linguistic difficulties of understanding what death is, but there is a more fundamental level at which we experience death, and it is worth consideration. At its most basic, how does the human brain conceive of and respond to death and the feeling of grief that it inspires? You might be surprised to discover that a field of study has been given over to this question – the neuroscience of grief and bereavement. In 2003, Professor of Psychosomatic Medicine & Psychotherapy Harald Gündel and his team performed a 'Functional Neuroanatomy of Grief', an MRI study to compare brain imaging in bereaved women. In their conclusions, they found that grief was

Grieving Family, from the collection of Steve DeGenero.

'mediated' by a widely distributed neural network rather than a single part of the brain. It involved memory retrieval, visual imagery, autonomic regulation and more. In other words, grieving involves an entire network of the brain, and this network functions differently in different people. Of course, as with all attempts to map the brain, neuroimaging doesn't give us the full picture: it tells us only that our brains light up in multiple ways, not what this might actually mean in terms of human experience. Our responses are just as – perhaps far more – important, because we are creatures of context. What neuroimaging does offer is an analogy. Just as death is both process and event, dying is both a personal and a communal activity. Metaphorically speaking, it takes an expansive network functioning together to respond to death. Essentially, then, in dying – and in knowing that we die – we are among friends, connected in that sense to human culture past and present.

The loss and recovery of grief ritual

Despite this privileged (or cursed) awareness of our mortality, and despite the fact that death is a constant across all cultures, many people still don't think about death until it happens. By that point, when hopes of healing have fallen away and the newly bereaved feel exhausted and alone, it may well be simplest to follow the usual pattern of subsequent events, without stopping to consider whether or not it feels helpful or responsive to your needs. The only reason I was able to see (and so to question) the rituals surrounding my grandfather's funeral was because they struck me as *unfamiliar*. We usually cannot get outside our own heads to see with fresh eyes; and even if we feel that we don't have the right tools with which to mourn our dead, we certainly don't have time to wrestle with new tools in the moment. This is why multicultural and historical perspectives are so valuable. They unmoor us so that we can look back from a distance and see more of the picture, not just about death, but about grieving. In the chapters that follow, we'll look at the far away and long ago, because there is no surer route to seeing ourselves anew. If we in the West seem today to be at a loss about how to approach death and its aftermath, why not explore how another culture has grappled with those same questions?

I will begin with a case from Cambodia, where dreams of the dead provided a new means of grieving in a nation torn by war. Devon Hinton, of Harvard, works a great deal with Cambodians suffering post-traumatic stress disorder (PTSD) after the Pol Pot period, 1975–9 (during which more than a million people perished). Those who survived had witnessed horrific deaths, the natural cycle of life had been completely interrupted and they had developed a unique way of grieving as a result. As Hinton explains, remorse and longing sometimes continue long after death, especially when the death was violent and is accompanied by painful memories. Worse, the Cambodians were denied their usual outlets for grief. Execution was frequent, even for the slightest offence (such as stealing a piece of fruit), and bodies were typically dumped in massive pits. It was rare that relatives could find their deceased loved ones among so many dead (something that is also true of plague conditions in the past, which I talk about in Chapter Three). When they could locate them, they were prohibited from performing traditional mortuary rituals because Pol Pot banned religious practice.

Cambodians believe that dreams are powerful, and that they result from the dreamer's own soul wandering free of the body at night. If they dream of a dead loved one, that means their soul has encountered the soul of someone deceased, and that this person has not been able to move on. To help the dead, certain burial and post-burial rituals must be performed. Otherwise, the dead remain stuck at one spiritual level. Because of Pol Pot, the entire population, in their time of need, had lost key elements of their grief culture, their means of dealing with death. With so many violent and unaccounted-for deaths, how were they to handle the loss of that grieving period? To do so, they eventually created a new ritual, called *chaa bangsegoul*, explicitly to deal with genocide. All the urns at the temple are taken out and put on a table, and participants can bring a picture of the dead or conjure them in their minds. The monks chant for three hours and then anoint the urns with lustral water. The ceremony gives blessing to *all* the deceased conjured in the ceremony. The Cambodian culture changed to make room for grief and death in a new way, incorporating a new ritual to heal over a devastating loss. May this serve not only as a lesson about death, but a lesson about hope. Collectively, a society may consciously decide to change the way it responds to even such a major event as death.

Of course, societies are changing all the time; it's just that we can't always see it happening in real time, and to be honest, we aren't always very good at accepting it. Our lives and experiences become our only reality. I mentioned before the house with two porches that my grandmother lived in. It was the whole world to me; nothing existed before that house. It had roots in eternity, and was as changeless and necessary to the movement of stars and planets as the sun around which we were dizzily spinning. When she and my grandfather announced that they were moving, it was as shocking to me as a universe out of balance. How could they? It was beyond the scope of my imagination to suppose they'd had a house *before* this one, just as I couldn't imagine them being children once like me. As we age, we get better at understanding how fleeting some traditions may be – but not a *lot* better. Did you know that embalming the dead in the US only became widely practised because of the Civil War and the need to transport bodies long distances? Did you know that public cemeteries (as we know them) were not invented in the US and UK until the nineteenth century? Did you know that the original funeral parlour was *the parlour*, a room in your own home, not a building designated specifically for funerary practice? Our changing culture also changes much of what happens after death. Some of these changes are good and necessary, like the changes to grief rituals enacted by the Cambodians. Others might not be so helpful, such as the taboo that can make death hard to approach or talk about in the West. It's important to explore what we lose or gain in the exchange.

The Loss of Sadness, published in 2007 by Allan Horwitz and Jerome C. Wakefield, begins with a useful comparison. The period after World War II was called an 'age of anxiety' in response to the horrors of warfare. An entire generation reeled, suffering what was considered a natural response to circumstance. Our present age, by contrast, might be called an 'age of depression', and the substitution of that single word makes all the difference. The anxiety of the early twentieth century had been considered 'normal', in the light of external events, whereas depression in the twenty-first century is understood as a diagnosable condition, an illness, a sickness of soul that should be (and often is) medicated.

Depression affects many people, making it difficult to get out of bed and do even the smallest task. We are lucky to live in an age that recognises it and treats it, especially since it seems to be on the rise. In the US, the diagnosis and treatment of depression increased by 300 per cent between 1987 and 1997. In Germany, rates rose by 70 per cent, and the total number of people in England suffering from depression for 2010 stood at 4.7 million. Similar studies have been published about France, Sweden and Italy – but also Japan, Taiwan, Lebanon and Russia. What might explain the huge increases? And what do these figures have to do with this book? Good questions.

Unlike blood disorders, cancer or other diseases, depression is diagnosed by its symptoms. Whether or not you are 'depressed' hinges on these symptoms as laid out by the *Diagnostic and Statistical Manual* or DSM:

Depressed mood or irritable most of the day, nearly
   every day
Decreased interest or pleasure in most activities, most of
   each day

Significant weight change (5 per cent) or change in
   appetite
Insomnia or hypersomnia
Change in activity level: psychomotor agitation or
   retardation
Fatigue or loss of energy
Feelings of worthlessness or excessive or
   inappropriate guilt
Diminished ability to think or concentrate, or more
   indecisiveness
Thoughts of death or suicide, or has suicide plan

But in the dazed and uncertain aftermath of death, when the funeral is over and you must return in some measure to your life, who hasn't felt empty, numb and even angry? In the weeks after losing my grandfather, I remember being furious with the world for not noticing that mine had been shattered. He had been a second father to me; I had lived with him. How dare the cashier smile at me – how dare the couple in the next booth giggle that way – how dare anyone expect anything but my frustration and rage? I was only seventeen, but the same experience recurred later when I lost my grandmother, and when my father suffered a life-threatening heart attack, and when my mother was diagnosed with cancer. I've even felt that way, to a lesser degree, at the loss of a beloved pet (frequently our very first loss as young people). Similarly, in the weeks and months after the death of someone close to you, decreased interest in activities, trouble sleeping, lethargy and inability to concentrate can mar attempts to get back to work or home life.

You might be horrified if the phone rings. You might be more horrified if it doesn't. Many of us go to work in a fog, scarcely able to think of anything besides the death of our loved one, and the only moments more painful are when we briefly forget they have died. In clinical terms, such symptoms could be classified as evidence of depression. But the difference is this: depression is a disorder, and dis-order, by its very definition, means *something is wrong with you*. And this can be a problem if applied to grief over death.

For most of recorded medical history, clinical and common understanding saw sadness *with a cause* and sadness *without a cause* as very different things. One constituted 'normal' grief and the other an 'abnormal' condition. The second condition was called melancholy. By the eighteenth and nineteenth centuries, this melancholy had begun to take on an identity, and even a literal 'face'. Etienne Esquirol, a French psychiatrist at the turn of the nineteenth century, had a series of drawings made to illustrate these features. Note the drawn brows and body language in the image on page 36; this kind of physical documentation proliferated, but was, unfortunately, rather vague. Western medicine has – for more than a century – created new classifications, and all the while distinguished between the two kinds of sadness. But in the twenty-first century, and in the very DSM diagnostic criteria, that isn't necessarily the case. According to the diagnostic manual, grief becomes diagnosable as depression if the symptoms are felt without cause – or with cause, but for too long. How long is too long? For bereavement, the DSM defines a 'normal' period of sadness to be *two months*.

Two months. Eight weeks, roughly, not even time enough

Drawing from *Des maladies mentales* (1838)
by Etienne Esquirol.

to raise a plant from seed to fruit. For other kinds of sadness, the DSM gives only two weeks, barely a vacation's worth of response time to things as difficult as divorce or job loss, etc. I don't mean to pick apart psychiatric categories – we need them. They have a place. The problem lies in the concept of 'normal'. Medical knowledge is frequently privileged as more accurate and more important than other forms of understanding or experience. This is especially true in the US, though also of the UK and much of Western Europe. When medical authorities tell us that two weeks or two months is sufficient, it creates a cultural expectation that grieving is, firstly, a short process with recognisable steps, and secondly, something that we must get over in order to return to 'normal'.

Those of us who have grieved know better. Our history and our neighbour cultures can prove the first assumption false. In Victorian England the stages of grief were specific and lengthy; a year was not too long for mourning a husband – and Queen Victoria herself, when widowed, wore mourning dress for the rest of her life. Among the Cambodians, the Arunta, the Borneo and certain groups from the African and Asian continents, death is understood as a long-running process that continues after the 'event' of death itself, and grieving is a part of that.

The second assumption is equally flawed. There is no 'normal'. And if there were, there would be no returning to it after the death of a loved one. Such losses are more like amputations. We carry them always; the world is changed after loss. And so it should be. The challenge is how to respond properly to that change.

The Cambodians lost their access to proper grieving rituals because of a force from without, pressuring and prohibiting them. Their response was to create new rituals to celebrate the dead and to attempt, however painfully, to resume life in the face of death. The problem for many of us in the West is that the pressure comes from within. If society demands that we process grief in record time or face the stigma of being 'disordered', we put incredible demands upon ourselves to conform. Screening for depression is ubiquitous in the West; Horwitz and Wakefield go so far as to call it the *surveillance of sadness*. From billboards to take-away quizzes in magazines, online checklists, WebMD and the DSM itself, we are confronted again with the paradox of the eternal versus the disposable. We are all expecting death, and death is forever – but at the same time we live in a society in which grief may be medicalised, even pathologised, and we often are ill-equipped to progress through it. It's no wonder so many of us don't slow down for grief, no wonder we march on, listless and uncertain, thirsty and unsatisfied. The traditional outlets for bereavement that existed a few generations ago (counselling by a priest or pastor, public exhibition of mourning, community-supported funerals and the comfort of the funerary rituals themselves) no longer seem plausible to many. Though we continue to reflect upon and so to tweak ritual traditions for weddings, christenings and other celebrations, the fact that we don't usually take time to reflect on death until it happens to someone we love may leave us struggling to get by on auto-pilot. In the US and UK (and much of Europe), the funeral takes place quite soon after death, so soon that there isn't time to consider adopting new rituals. Without time to think and discuss them beforehand, they cannot necessarily serve as meaningful rites by which to come to terms with death, grief and loss. Thus many of us in the West are stuck: finding the conventional funeral rites and rituals brief or unsatisfying, even shallow, but unable to find a better way without advance preparation. And then there is the question of what to do *after* the funeral – the point where, for many, there is a realisation that it does not – cannot – provide an end to the process of death as we may, perhaps unconsciously, have expected.

Of course the funeral cannot really mark the conclusion of the grieving process. It is frequently only the beginning.

Death as the enemy

The loss (or at least the abridgement) of our grief culture explains something else, too: the increasingly popular focus on stalling death entirely and living in a medically extended eternity. In 1912, medical biologist and Nobel Prize winner Alexis Carrel stated that 'Death is not necessary . . . [it is] merely a contingent phenomenon.' In 2009, Kurzweil (the 'thinking machine') said much the same thing, suggesting that nanobots will one day rebuild our cells synthetically from the inside out. American molecular geneticist Bill Andrews added weight to the idea in 2011 when he discovered a supplement for reprogramming cells. In his theory, if you could stop DNA strings called 'telomeres' from shortening, you would also lengthen your life. These erstwhile predictions promise eternal or vastly extended life, but not for our generation; these far-flung ideas have receding deadlines. Meanwhile, our current medical technology holds out something less miraculous but still coveted: extended life, replacement parts and – failing all else – life support systems. *Never say die* seems to be the mantra, never surrender. The healthy are encouraged not to think about illness; the ill not to think about death, but to fight long and hard for life. There is nothing wrong per se with the fighting spirit, of course. But it puts yet more pressure on those whose lives are expiring, and upon their kith and kin.

In an article critiquing the 'survivor narrative' so frequently forced upon the cancer patient, Mark A. Lewis, MD, explains that 'the patient, as a victim, is expected to put on a bold face in the midst of their vulnerability.' The metaphor of hard-fought battle has become so usual, says Lewis, that rarely do we see an obituary of a cancer patient that doesn't mention their lost 'battle' against the disease. But of course, many do die – and if they feel obliged to avoid speaking about death for fear of giving quarter to the enemy, or to remain upbeat in the face of increasingly long odds, that can make the finality of death all the more crushing. Humanity distinguishes itself by expecting death, and yet it still comes unexpected. Contemporary Western culture is built on denial and fear of death rather than acceptance of and preparation for it. But this view is actually rather recent. Most westerners, for most of our history, did not share it. They were not caught between eternal and disposable; they were able to hold those two ideas, event and process, easily in their minds at once. Our ancestors, who did not have the luxury – or burden – of being able to deny death, instead lived with the acceptance of it. I would argue that such acceptance can bring unexpected benefits.

In December 2013, I wrote the introduction for a special issue of *Culture, Medicine, and Psychiatry* on narratives and medicine ('Meaning and Medicine in a New Key'). I began by quoting the *British Medical Journal* from 1911: 'Is there any relation between disease and literature? To this question we have no hesitation in answering, Yes. We go so far as to say that without disease, or physical disability of some kind, there would be very little literature.'

Is there, the BMJ asks, a relationship between disease and literature? Between mortality and mythos? Between death and storytelling? In answering yes, we raise a new question: how are these stories to be shared? The knowledge of death has given birth to some of the world's greatest traditions, stories, practices and beliefs. Sharing through storytelling, in addition to being a kind of ritual in itself, is also part of many other ritual means of preparing for death, whether as the first step on a long journey, or that journey's end. In Chapter Two, I will explore the stories – and rituals – of seven other cultures as a way of helping to contextualise my own.

A useful example of the power of stories as rituals comes from trauma treatment. In March 2012, *Culture, Medicine, and Psychiatry* published the work of Wozniak and Allen about a shelter for abused women in Montana. Care workers had trouble helping their patients to move beyond the trauma they had experienced. Despite extensive counselling, the women frequently found themselves returning to their abusers or moving on to new partners who were similarly abusive. Confounded and frustrated, the shelter psychologists decided to incorporate rites of passage (similar to those practised by Native Americans) into therapy. Women participated in several ceremonies, one of which had them writing down their weaknesses, their 'old selves', and then dropping them into a swift-flowing river. Using this and other rituals, the women let their trauma go symbolically, and one by one they were able to move on with their lives. The women did not necessarily believe in an indigenous worldview, but they did not have to. The rituals themselves had the power to heal.

It is often easier to understand concepts like these by looking outward. By looking at the rituals and death practices of other cultures, as in the story above, we can approach the history of Western ideas about death and dying. Distance is important, not because it prevents us from facing death head-on, but because it gives us the space to see the subject in its full complexity, as well as all the many ways in which we can approach it. In this sense, art is a useful and beautiful medium. It allows us to transcend our fears and our cultural barriers. By listening to others' stories and practices, we get a better understanding of how and why we respond to death, what it means to us and how grief can help us to accept it.

This is what it means to be expecting death *not* as the end of life, but as part of it.

Chapter 2

EAT YOUR DEAD (AND OTHER ADVICE)

Death and the departed
across the globe

A procession makes its way along a high ridge in the mountains. Dressed in bright colours, the participants beat hand-held drums by turning them side to side in rhythm. The steady *plok-plok* is accompanied by the ringing of bells and the singing of chants that echo in the thin air of high altitude. Above them, as if in expectation, soar a host of griffon vultures. This slow-marching party and its feathered heralds head for a sacred cliff at the roof of the world; for this is Tibet, and this is a funeral.

Regardless of where we live or who we are, it is both sensible and expedient to prepare for death. Historically, this was a problem of space and health as well as grief and loss. While our ancestors had to bear the burden of sorrow for a missing friend just as we must do, they also had to deal with pressing practical concerns – such as, *what do we do with the body?* To leave it lying out would attract animal life and pestilence; to burn it would use fuel; to bury it would require workable soil. And so, across the world, burial differs markedly due to climate and geography as well as spiritual practice and cultural assimilation.

When a loved one dies, we have channels that we work through. Call the physician, call the funeral director – call those for whom this is business and not tragedy. But it wasn't always so, and still isn't so today for many people. What might we in the West learn from approaching death through the eyes of another culture? By examining the death practices of cultures unfamiliar to us – that is, death 'out there' – we can begin to approach death in a new way 'in here'.

There's a danger in examining 'the other' as though walking through a cabinet of curiosities, of course. Labelling a list of practices as merely bizarre, weird or creepy does no one any good. *But what if something really is shockingly strange to you?* Then let us draw nearer. The more foreign a custom seems, the more useful the moment of contact. To look into the strange and find the familiar is also to understand one's own self more clearly. The very unfamiliarity causes us to reflect in turn on our own 'normal' practices. In what ways are we carrying out grief rituals that bear the fingerprint of our cultural roots, our geographical or geopolitical loci, our spiritual and human need for closure in light of life's final event? Death rituals are sacred, part of our lived experience, and they should be deeply meaningful. Looking at both familiar and previously unencountered grief rituals can transform the way we think about mortality and our responses to it. Death, when kept so near, ceases to threaten us, ceases to be alien. Ritual, when embraced, can be the means to healing and to progressing through grief for the living who remain.

After all, understanding is built through exploration and comparison.

Death in transition: sky burials

Tibetan Buddhists practise 'sky burial', the tradition of ritually dissecting the dead into small pieces and giving the remains to birds. This may seem undignified to us – but it is far from it. Sky burial not only solves the practical concern of removing a body in the cold, tree-less mountains, it agrees with the fundamental core of their cultural beliefs. Located in the Himalayas, Tibet has a diverse ethnic population which practises more than one religion, though Tibetan Buddhism remains primary. For Buddhists, the cycle of birth, death and rebirth is crucial to understanding our present life. Though different branches of Buddhism understand these cycles differently and have different sacred texts, all follow the teachings of Siddhartha Gautama (the Buddha). Reflection on death among Buddhists relates to Siddhartha's 'four sights' – of a sick man, an old man, a dead man and an ascetic (someone who abstains and is highly self-disciplined). He renounces his royal lineage as a result of these sights, choosing moral discipline as a way of overcoming death. Though some aspects of Buddhism still consider the divine, Buddha himself is not thought to be a god. Rather, he is a figure who attained *nirvana*. Nirvana is a difficult concept to grasp, but it says a great deal about the Buddhist perspective on death. Traditional Buddhist ideas see life as cyclical, following the doctrine of *samsara*, which literally means 'wandering' from one life to the next. Not all lives are equal, however! No one wants to be reborn as a lowly animal – a dog, a pig, a snake. The object is to ascend in the chain of being, and this is achieved through *karma*. As Michael Coogan, professor emeritus of religious studies at Stonehill College and lecturer at Harvard Divinity School, explains, karma is best thought of as a 'law of moral retribution'. To rise, however, also means to humble oneself, to be free of desires and

Yama, the Lord of Death, holding the Wheel of Life.

liberated from earthly attachments. Nirvana is achieved when desire ceases and karma is exhausted, but this means an end to rebirth. When Buddha achieved nirvana, he ceased to exist.

To Buddhists, death is both the beginning of rebirth and also a final embracing of non-existence. Preparation for this cycle begins in life, but continues into death. Funerals are intended to assist the departed soul to a better rebirth, but Tibetan funerals go further still. Buddhist meditation master

Chögyam Trungpa Rinpoche explains it best by suggesting that the *Tibetan Book of the Dead* could also reasonably be called the *Tibetan Book of Birth*. Over a period of forty-nine days, a lama (religious person) chants from the book over and over, frequently in front of the corpse, but after burial, they will chant over a picture or memento. So important are the first days of this chant that mourners in the West, where the body is turned over to a mortician, may ask that a recording be played in the funeral home where the body resides. Why? Because the book tells the departed soul how to seek nirvana, or, if nirvana isn't possible, how to gain a good rebirth. It is truly a book *of* and *for* the dead, a text that marks the long journey where all lives are connected and intertwine. From the Main Verses:

> Now when the bardo of the moment before death dawns
>   upon me,
> I will abandon all grasping, yearning and attachment,
> Enter undistracted into clear awareness of the teaching,
> And eject my consciousness into the space of the unborn mind;
> As I leave this compound body of flesh and blood
> I will know it to be a transitory illusion.

According to Trungpa Rinpoche, death is hardly even seen as an irritation in Tibetan culture, even if it remains an event of sadness and loss for those who remain. The greatest kindness the living can do for the dying is to be honest about their approaching death, and then to help guide them – alive and dead – towards liberation from the cycle of rebirth. In the meantime, however, the living must do something more. Tibetan Buddhists believe all lives are connected to each other and to the earth. Once the dead have been prepared, they must be returned to that earth as quickly as possible, becoming once more part of other living things.

Let us return to the mountain. Do-Tarap, Tibet is one of the most remote places on earth at 12,000 feet. The body is washed by loving relatives and then wrapped in a colourful cloth. A procession of praying, chanting and music travels more than an hour away from town with the community's lama, and also the man responsible for carrying out the sky burial. The family carries the body; the man carries sharpened knives. What happens next may seem alien and brutal to Western eyes, but is both spiritually and environmentally important. The undertaker will unwrap the body while ritual prayers are spoken or sung from afar. While this is going on, vultures and birds of prey gather in the sky, circling and waiting for the ritual dissection. The body will, by these means, be broken down for easier consumption by the birds, whose lives will be enriched by the person's flesh and blood. Scarcely anything will be left, and nothing wasted. The soul has moved on to the next stage, awaiting rebirth; the body – as a vessel – has been made to serve a new purpose.

The Tibetan Buddhists' practice only looks unusual to a Western perspective because it is unfamiliar. Then again, just how different is it? In the US, UK and other parts of Europe, funerals include their own sort of undertaker or mortician. In many cases, bodies are opened, drained, embalmed (sometimes for viewing) and then interred in earth or vaults (there is also the possibility of organ donation, where vital organs are removed beforehand for use by others). In both cases, there is preparation of the body and a re-commitment to the earth of beloved remains. Dying is harder in the West, says Trungpa Rinpoche, because the truth of death is hidden from us. In that truth, even if it seems brutal, is a kind of peace and beauty – and on the high ridges of the Himalayan plateau, it's perhaps easier to see why.

Grief as rage, skulls as vessels

Understanding death as a transition does not – and should not – mean that the living feel less sorrow. The few sky burials that have been filmed, and the anthropologists who have been able to witness them, report the same grief-stricken sobs that attend any bitter loss. Knowing that a loved one is moving to another world or plane doesn't make the mourner less lonely or destitute in *this* one. As a result, the frequent consolation *they are in a better place* can be little comfort to the bereaved.

The British journalist and author Virginia Ironside once discussed rage in an article for the *Independent*. 'Nearly every book on bereavement enraged me,' she laments. 'I was in utter turmoil . . . with other shameful feelings of rage, greed, loathing, hatred for life.' In the model developed by psychiatrist Elisabeth Kübler-Ross, anger appears as a 'stage of grief', a stopping point on the way to 'healing' (the order is: denial, anger, bargaining, depression, acceptance). But what happens when the stages are not in order? Or one lasts too long? What if there is no healing, but only a basic functioning after the supposed stages are over? A basic Google search will reveal an astounding number of books and websites about grief and how it's supposed to work; one of these – 4Therapy.com – helpfully explains that there are no rules for grief, but also makes the following statement: a grief that lasts too long is an 'extreme version of the normal feelings', resulting in survivor guilt, extreme agitation, intense sensitivity and intrusive thoughts. Understandably, this idea aligns with the DSM and its categories of abnormal grief and depression, and the horribly problematic concept of 'normal' grief. Tellingly, however, a similar search of the terms 'grief' and 'rage' turns up very little. Anger may be a stage of grief, but we aren't *really* supposed to feel rage . . . are we?

Among the Ilongot people of the Northern Philippines, it was common to headhunt – literally to kill and behead rivals, during the 'rage of bereavement'. Given the unusual and unusually violent nature of this ritual, anthropologist Renato

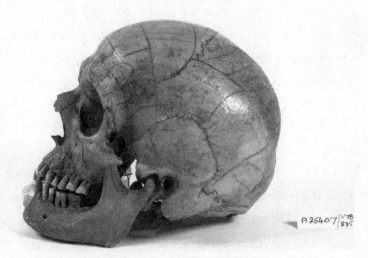

An engraved human phrenology skull.

Rosaldo went looking for explanations. What he found was the root of his own cultural assumptions.

Rosaldo worked among the Ilongot people, a tribe of the southern Sierra Madre, in the 1960s and 1970s. His wife Michelle, a psychological anthropologist, also participated in fieldwork, and the two of them wrote extensively about the habits and customs of Ilongot (including their relative sexual equality). The most unusual and alarming tradition concerned 'grief rage'. After a death, men in the village felt compelled – irresistibly driven – to headhunt. The hunters endure hunger, thirst and deprivation in the weeks it takes to set up an ambush; because they must wait for their prey to happen along, the process is lengthy and non-specific. When at last they have attacked, killed and beheaded the hapless victim, the Ilongot do not keep the head as a trophy or bring it back home. *They throw it away.* How could any of this help in the grieving process? How could death be mitigated by more death?

When Rosaldo asked the tribesmen what drove them to the practice, they claimed that severing and throwing away a head was the same as throwing away the anger at death. The head becomes something 'to carry' their anger away, a vessel for grief-born rage. To Rosaldo, this description didn't really solve the problem, though; or not at first. What caused the rage to begin with? Was it life-for-life? The description given by the Ilongot was too simple, or even naive, he thought. Rosaldo tried different questions, prying further into their cultural traditions, but came up with the same thing each time. Rage was born of grief, said the headhunters. Death literally gave birth to the practice. Problematically for the Ilongot, however, the government outlawed headhunting. The traditional ways had been blocked (just as the Pol Pot period blocked traditional burial for the Cambodians). Few avenues remained. Rosaldo describes the painful position of a man who lost his seventh child, a six-month-old baby. Shortly after the death, the father converted to evangelical Christianity (which was being introduced to the area by missionaries). Rosaldo admits to reading the situation all wrong; he originally thought that the grieving father sought a new religion in the belief that it would *prevent* more deaths. The Ilongot corrected him: what the man sought wasn't denial of death (the typical Western response), but a means of coping with death's reality. What he needed was a ritual, for his own had been taken away. He needed a new means of 'carrying' his rage away before it destroyed him.

Where do you put it, incredible, all-consuming grief? We all need to vent, to put our grief somewhere, to do something. Casting ashes of the dead upon the waters – or commemorating them with a book or memoir, a photo album, a scholarship, a community centre – these may, in their own way, be similar vehicles for grief. While westerners may never come to terms with the concept of murder-for-grief, it begins to illuminate the common plight of our human condition. Rituals, when understood and embraced, can be the means to healing for the living, and may even be a means of connection between disparate cultures. Though Renato failed fully to grasp the meaning of the Ilongot conception of death during his time with them, he did come to understand it at last – through his own grief.

In 1981, Michelle Rosaldo fell to her death while researching among the tribes of Luzon, Philippines. It was a moment in time: she lost her footing on the ridge and fell 65 feet into a swift-flowing river. Renato himself found her body. What were the emotions that wracked him in this most terrible of all moments? What were the doubts? He describes the experience in an essay years later: 'How could she abandon me? How could she be so stupid as to fall?' It was not sadness – or not only sadness. It was *rage*. We often say that our world changes after a death like that. But it does not only change; it rocks, it heaves, it shatters. It breaks and bends and twists. The bereaved is like a shaken leaf on roiling waters, and there is nothing at all you can do about it, nothing you can change. A thousand questions may crowd your mind at a time like this: why did we come here? Why wasn't I standing there? Or more drastically world-shifting questions: why did we choose this career? Why did we have to travel? Why didn't we stay safe at home? There is a human desire for someone to be at fault. Sometimes we blame the victim. Sometimes we blame ourselves. But the horrid wound gapes and pulls all the while. The Ilongot had a custom that recognised rage and gave it a place and a temporality (that is, a beginning and an end). This tradition was taken from them. Renato Rosaldo came from a perspective that rarely, if ever, recognises rage as a legitimate response to death in the first place. In a moment, he understood that the Ilongot explanation did not need to be more complex: the 'anger at abandonment is irreducible in that nothing at a deeper level explains it'. Death 'births' rage because at some fundamental, wordless level, rage is the gut-wrenching passion of the soul, gnashing its teeth in the dark.

The guidelines on stages of grief, the websites about

bereavement support and the DSM are correct in saying that we can't *stay* in a place of extreme anger. The Ilongot knew that. Renato Rosaldo knew that. The task: when we have prepared the body, how do we put away the grief? How do we continue knowing and honouring the lost loved one without the pain of loss consuming us?

Consuming grief – and eating the dead

I can recall the first time I heard of necrophagy. It was in an anthropology class. My response mirrors, I think, most westerners' first reaction to the practice: 'I'm sorry, what? They *eat* their *dead?*'

The biological imperative for most species is to avoid death, or even the scene of death. Charnel houses, collections of bones, places of decay, even the smell of decay alert us that pestilence and predators may follow. The vultures and birds of prey that attend a sky burial evolved specifically for this function – but why would any human want to cannibalise the dead?

The Wari live in the rainforests of Brazil. Until as late as 1960, they disposed of dead bodies primarily through mortuary cannibalism. To the Wari, this practice symbolised their deep respect and honour of their loved ones – but it also allowed them to deal with the loss. The funeral engages the whole community; the dead man lies on a mat, painted red and starting to bloat in the heat. Mourners walk round and round, wailing in sorrow and also to frighten unfriendly spirits away. They are not going to bury this body, however. The body is about to be dismembered and roasted for consumption.

Anthropologist Beth Conklin describes the scene as reaching a 'fevered pitch' before the body is first cut open. Mourners pile together, struggling to hold the body or to press themselves to it in grief for the coming separation. The men of the village begin dismemberment, removing organs first and then severing the head and cutting the joints before placing limbs upon the roasting rack (inedibles, like hair and entrails, are burned). The elders of the village explain that only the cutting of the body is emotionally difficult – to eat the remains, on the other hand, is good and right. The meat is not eaten from bones, but cut up, almost ritually, and placed on clean mats. Only relatives (but not immediate relations – spouses or children) eat the body, usually the dead person's in-laws. They eat slowly, weeping while eating. As Conklin explains, they must consume all or most of the body. Not being able to do so would be offensive; if the body had decayed too much to stomach, eaters would swallow parts and then cremate the rest at dawn the next day. When the rest of the body had been cremated, the ashes would be buried and the area swept clean. As with the sky burial, nothing remains of the funeral rites or the body.

Why consume the dead? The living Wari explain that they would rather be incorporated into the living bodies of their kin than rot in the cold, wet ground. Even their ashes will typically be buried under the house sleeping platform, close to the living and the warmth of fire and life. The cycle of life continues through the eating of the dead. Conklin relates a Wari consumption/life-cycle story about the maize (corn) spirit:

one man walked along a path and dropped a kernel of maize on the ground. It cried out, but the man didn't hear and went on. Another man saw the kernel and, in sympathy, ate it. When the two men planted their fields, only the maize-eater's crops came up. Without eating, there is no saving, no preserving, no rebirth. Moreover, the Wari claim that dismembering and consuming the body disperses and dissipates the grief. They have all shared the death, and in eating the remains, they shed their grief and anger. Necro-cannibalism can be dangerous (certain diseases are transmitted only through the eating of brain tissue, for instance), but for the Wari's grief culture, eating your dead ensured health and safety, a way of keeping the dead near you. And believe it or not, both Eastern and Western culture practised a version of necrophagy, in the form of corpse medicine, from the Renaissance to the Victorian era.

Corpse medicine doesn't sound very healthful, I'll agree, but the dead body was once considered a source of healing. In Rome, the fresh blood of slain gladiators was thought to be a cure for epilepsy, and famed physician Claudius Galen recommended body parts and fluids as a means of fighting disease as late as 200 AD. Richard Sugg, author of *Mummies, Cannibals, Vampires: The History of Corpse Medicine from the Renaissance to the Victorians*, suggests that mummies were very popular as medicine, too, and might be used in plasters to treat everything from snake-bite to syphilis. Powdered skull made frequent appearances in tonics and pharmacy recipes, as did distillations of blood (Mary Roach speaks to some of this in *Stiff*, along with a case of allegedly 'human' dumplings, where dutiful Chinese daughters-in-law would prepare dishes with bits of their own flesh for an ailing parent). One of the more infamous cases in the West concerns the life of Pope Innocent VIII in 1492. In an attempt to save his life, the physician bled three young men to death and gave their blood – still warm – to the ailing Pope. It did not work, except, perhaps, to make Innocent's name highly ironic at the moment of his death a few days later. Corpse medicine continued well into Elizabethan England and even during the Victorian era, and was practised both in the West and in the East. For followers of those earlier medicinal trad-itions, as for the Wari, the body, even in death, was life-giving.

Eating the dead means taking part in the wheel of life inti-mately, while also dispersing the grief and rage felt among a community's members. We in the West are unlikely to pursue this line of thought, but neither should we rush to judge it as defiling, disrespectful or impure. Here, as elsewhere, the unfa-miliar means of disposal is only shocking because each of us is so near our own traditions that we can scarcely see outside them – and this is as true for the Wari as for anyone else. When asked repeatedly why they practised this ritual, the response was always one of surprise. *Why wouldn't we? It's what we've always done.* Ideally all death rituals should serve equally to quell the rage and disperse the grief, making death more approach-able by making it familiar once more.

The dead are always with us

I realise that notions of the dead remaining among us hold the possibility of being both promise and threat. The Western cultural fascination with zombies, mummies and vampires is ample proof, and other cultures' traditions (such as burning the house of the deceased or performing noisy rituals to ensure they don't come back) also bear witness to our combined hope and fear of the departed. The vampire, says Paul Barber, author of *Vampires, Burial and Death*, is but a local manifestation of a worldwide phenomenon: the revenant as a means of explaining death. The term 'revenant' usually refers to an animated corpse rather than a ghost – a physical body, sometimes with the signs of decay and sometimes not, depending on the folklore. In most cases, however, these creatures are far from benign. Vampires hunt the living, according to tradition, and their bites are infectious. They are, in a manner, diseased bodies and contaminating ones. In other words, they appear to threaten the living in exactly the same way an ordinary dead body might: by being sites of potential pestilence. There is one rather obvious difference: dead bodies stay put, while undead bodies threaten to return. But for the moment, let's focus on the aspects that connect the revenant to death and disease: namely, the combination of the familiar and the unfamiliar.

How to distinguish the proper, familiar dead from the unfamiliar undead? During the eighteenth century, Europe witnessed a vampire scare resulting in the appointment of vampire commissioners, autopsy inquests and the occasional mutilation of corpses – the position and condition of skeletons unearthed in Český Krumlov (and dated to 1732) suggest that vampire-killing rituals had been performed. Barber lists a number of characteristics gleaned from the *Visum et Repertum* (from the words 'to see' and 'discover'), a kind of post-mortem report written that same year by military surgeon Johann Flückinger after a mass exhumation:

> 'Suspected vampires do not show appropriate amounts
>   of decay (or none at all) in comparison to the
>   bodies nearby
> There is fresh blood or liquid on the body
> Hair and nails appear to have grown
> Bodies appeared ruddy or bloated with blood'

Much of this can be attributed to misunderstanding the process of decay and the effects of the time of year. But although by 1755 Gerhard van Swieten, personal physician of Empress Maria Theresa of Austria, concluded that 'vampires only appear where ignorance still reigns', he did little to change the minds of locals. To them, the revenant represented a death that spreads, a death that makes once-familiar friends and family into potential threats to body and soul. The process of decay itself is horribly 'othering', in that it remakes those well-known forms and figures into something utterly alien, where boundaries of identity (as of body) dissolve.

The responses to such self-obliterating processes vary by culture and time period, but the drive to 're-familiarise' death remains common. One means of stopping the alienation is to stop the decay itself. The word 'mummy' comes from the Persian word for bitumen, an asphalt-like substance, likely in reference to the dark resin covering Egyptian remains – and the mummies of Egypt are frequently the first that come to mind. However, mummification has been practised on every continent, from Japan's self-mummified monks to the Chinchorro people of the Atacama Desert in Peru and Chile. A body mysteriously preserved from decay may spark fears, but a body intentionally preserved becomes a familiar relic, opening the possibility of keeping the dead near in beneficial (rather than threatening) ways – something to consider, given the prevalence of embalming in the American context.

Anthropologist Bernardo Arriaza says the early Chinchorro people followed an elaborate process, including the removal of organs (like the Egyptians). They also packed the bodies with clay and sewed the skin on before painting them black. The Atacama Desert is one of the driest climates on earth, and so mummification would have happened to a degree anyway. Ecologist Pablo Marquet suggests that the Chinchorro would have seen dead bodies, dried and preserved, frequently exposed by wind. As a result, he explains, 'dead people became a very significant part of the physical landscape of the living, and also the psychological landscape of the living people'. Intentionally preserving them, and by means of paint and wigs and preservation processes rendering them recognisable, made the natural process part of ritual and so also of lived experience. In some cases 'the faces have been repainted several times', suggesting that care was constantly taken of these bodies, possibly as acts of veneration.

The Toraja of Sulawesi, Indonesia, bury their dead in a variety of ways, sometimes hanging coffins from cliff-sides or interring remains inside of growing trees, or – occasionally – keeping them in the home. Life actually revolves around death for the Torajans, and wealth is amassed throughout life in order to ensure a properly auspicious send-off at death. Raising money can be a lengthy process, and so a family embalms and stores the body in the home until the funeral can be properly paid for. Until the ceremonies are complete, a Torajan is not considered truly 'dead', even if the process takes years. Instead, they are 'sick', and so symbolically fed and cared for (and even taken out and about) until the actual interment. Anthropologist Kelli Swazey considers the Torajan practice one that recognises 'that our relationships with other humans, their impact on our social reality, doesn't cease with the termination of the physical processes of the body, that there's a period of transition as the relationship between the living and the dead is transformed but not ended'. No longer an alien or unfamiliar process, death and the corpse are reintegrated with life and the living body. To the Torajans, death is familiar and even intimate.

The Torajans also practise a ritual called Ma'Nene, which may occur yearly or every few years. Anthropologist Jane C. Wellenkamp refers to it as a form of 'secondary' burial involving cleaning and repairing the gravesites and attending to the dead. Part of this care involves dressing the dead in new clothing and taking them around the village in parade, a celebration and type of extended family reunion. In 2012, the practice garnered some press in the *Daily Mail* and *Huffington Post* when pictures were published of the Torajan dead on parade. Taken up and reproduced on other sites, the images bore phrases like 'Zombies!' or 'Dead Walking!' – sensationalised scripts that say more about Western discomfort with the dead than about the practice itself. As Swazey is quick to point out, 'If we [in the West] could expand our definition of death to encompass life, we could experience death as part of life and perhaps face death with something other than fear.' Exhuming the dead does not, in this context, constitute a desecration, nor does it return us to the contagious terror of the revenant. Instead, the practice of disinterment serves as an excuse to celebrate the cycles of life.

Not every celebration is entirely without the threat of violence, however. Among the Merina of Madagascar, *famadihana* – or the rewrapping of the dead in new shrouds and dancing them through the streets – is both an act of celebration and veneration, and one that exists to placate ancestors so they do not bring harm to the living. David Graeber of the University of Chicago noted that, among rural communities, the presence of dead ancestors in the lives of their descendants 'made itself felt' through the constraint or violence the ancestors might choose to inflict. An example comes from a village fire, purportedly the result of failing to wrap three of the bodies during a famadihana festival – the community believed their inattention to the dead led to retribution by their angry spirits.

At the same time, however, there can be great respect and care displayed by the villagers, who rewrap the bodies and spray them with perfume before sitting among them, sometimes cradling them in their laps. Though the Wari no longer practise necro-cannibalism (the practice ceased after contact with missionaries and outsiders), for tribe members, dismemberment was more distressing than actual cannibalism. The still-practising Merina, however, often feel the most emotional shock *before* the rewrapping, and during a sharing process of offering the dead honey, rum or tobacco. While women generally hold the bodies, men are responsible for wrapping them

– first in one white sheet, then another, then in coloured silks. After the wrapping, the celebratory part of the process begins, with the people dancing vigorously and even violently with the ancestral remains. Tinged with aggression, the practice nonetheless makes the dead a considerable part of the Merina's lived experience – not in mourning, but in *dancing*.

Additional types of mummies exist the world over, including the Sokushinbutsu (self-mummified monks) of Dainichi temple in Japan. In mentioning this last group, I mean to return us to the Buddhist practice of self-denial and the acceptance (and even courting) of death. These Buddhist priests practised an extreme form of asceticism that would lead to their deaths, and yet also establish them as 'living Buddhas'. In addition to practising rigorous exercise to rid the body of fat, they consumed only nuts, berries, tree bark and pine needles while gradually reducing the amount they ate. According to Ken Jeremiah, who writes extensively about Japanese religion and martial arts, the practitioner would starve to death within ten years when the practice was successful. The priest would also drink a poisonous tea made from the urushi tree, causing loss of bodily fluids (a kind of pre-drying). Finally, he would lock himself into a tomb connected to a bamboo breathing tube. The tombs would be opened after three years, and, if the mummification was successful, the remains would be dressed in robes and worshipped by their loyal followers. Jeremiah recounts the story of Kūkai (also known as Kōbō Daishi). When he was seventy-two, he sealed himself in a mountain cave and meditated until his death. According to tradition, his hair continued to grow, so his followers returned every few years to trim it and provide new robes. As 'living Buddha', Kōbō Daishi had removed himself from the cycle of life and of need, achieving nirvana but also existing *between* life and death, between familiar and unfamiliar, in a stasis that required and permitted no change. In a sense, such preserved remains are *undead*, but again, unlike the revenants that haunted European imaginations, they exist as beneficent saints.

Loved, revered, cared for, these preserved bodies – the dead among us – render death less strange and more familiar. Why? It isn't due solely or even primarily to the fact that decay has been slowed. Death becomes familiar because of its celebrated communal nature, because the ancestor never leaves entirely but remains as part of the household in some form. Even more internationally recognisable festivals, like November's Day of the Dead in Mexico, with its brightly coloured skeletons and sugar skulls, serve as a celebratory reminder: bones are lovely in the eyes of kith and kin, and love drives away fear. The dead are always with us, so eat the communal dead-bread (*pan de muerto* for Day of the Dead) and dance with your ancestors; there are no vampires here.

Joining the celebration

The Wari eat the dead; the Torajans feed the dead; during the Mexican Day of the Dead festival, people eat *with* the dead (figuratively speaking). The point is not consumption but communion. In *Skulls to the Living, Bread to the Dead*, Stanley Brandes dates the earliest reference to 'Day of the Dead' to a document from the Barcelona silversmiths' guild, 1671. In referring to All Souls Day, celebrated by the Catholic Christians in the area, the document specifies that two *corteres of pa dels morts* (dead bread) be offered to the deceased. The practice is much older, however; a will from 1344 asked that heirs annually place 'five *sueldos* of bread, candles, and other obligatory objects' on the tomb. In general, these offerings are ritualistic; the dead are not actually expected to eat, but rather to enjoy the presence or aroma of the offerings. In later traditions, this 'dead bread' is then eaten by the living in honour of the dead and in celebration of life.

According to a study by Jesús Angel Ochoa Zazueta, offerings might include 'tamales, oranges, sugarcane, bananas, different types of pan de muerto, salt, water, candy, corn on the cob, lard, atole, squash, tejocotes [a small, yellow, plum-like fruit], lemons, sugar, chocolate, mole, cinnamon, corn kernels, tangerines, tall candles [cirios], votive candles and flowers'. There are two different perspectives on what a tradition of this kind means; one suggests that it is an embrace of death, and the other that it is a negation of death. During the festival, you might consume little coffins and skulls, turning them into sweet sugar as they melt in your mouth. Brandes asks if this process is itself a denial of death through the assertion of life, but this glosses over one very important point: life and death exist always together, like summer and winter. Whether the Day of the Dead embraces death or asserts life does not change one salient feature: this is a celebration, a serious occasion not to be taken lightly — but also a time of laughing and dancing.

For the Day of the Dead, Christian traditions from All Souls Day mix with folklore, ancient Aztec tradition and modern reimaginings and reinterpretations through art, food and song. In many respects, there is no single way the Mexican festival approaches death and this serves as a reminder: culture changes over time, and traditions change, too. Not all of the death, grief and burial rituals mentioned here are still practised. Some have passed away entirely (like headhunting your grief-rage) and are recorded only in anthropological narratives. These shifts do not mark the death of death culture, however. They prove that death rituals exist, in many respects, for the living who remain.

I began this chapter with a suggestion: that by examining the death practices of cultures foreign to us, we can see more clearly our own approach to death – and, more importantly, we can imagine ways that we might approach death differently in the future. As the customs of others become more familiar, our own practices begin to look ever so slightly less so. We can compare and ask questions. Why do we call strangers to take care of the body? Why are the final preparations for burial done by non-family members, in a place far away from the home? Why do we embalm the body if we don't plan to preserve it? Why do we gather for viewings and wakes? Why flowers – or eulogies – or processionals? Most of us in Western societies have never asked these questions. The answers, however, may surprise and move us. Sometimes one's own traditions can seem hollow, smaller and less vibrant than those taking place elsewhere, but often that is only because we are too near them to see properly. Sometimes the unfamiliar sparkles only because it seems new; we may find that our collective past holds the key to rituals that are richer than we thought. If we have, in fact, lost something that other cultures have retained, perhaps it is the meaning-making process of really thinking about and taking part in ritual. What if we investigated our own complex and varied past? In Chapter Three, it's time to turn the lens towards Western or European traditions through history to track our ever-evolving approach to death. By looking back, we may eventually be able to see further forward, past the obstacles that keep us from drawing nigh, that prohibit us from meeting death in a more intimate and less fearful manner. After all, death is, at its heart, a *living* culture – and subject to change.

Chapter 3

THROUGH A
GLASS, DARKLY

The changing view of death
and grief in the West

Paul Koudounaris photographs the dead. His work, culminating in brilliant image-driven books such as *Empire of Death* and *Heavenly Bodies*, features the articulated, opulently jewelled skeletons of the Roman catacombs, set in gold filigree wire. Responses to his work tend towards awe mixed with a kind of macabre wondering. Surely they must be thousands of years old – something akin to the mummies of Egypt? In truth, these decorated skeletons began to appear in the first half of the seventeenth century, primarily to reaffirm the Catholic Church's desire to venerate relics, but also to replace those that had been destroyed during the Reformation and to send a message about the glory that God reserved for those who stayed true. The adoration with which they were regaled served

Bejewelled skeleton from the Baroque era.

a cultural (and politico-religious) function in our not-so-distant past during a time of tremendous upheaval.

Dr Koudounaris's other work concerns a tradition still going on today, the *ñatitas* of La Paz, Bolivia (which occupy a section of his latest book, *Memento Mori*). These small 'household skulls' are carefully preserved and made part of the home in a similar way to the familiar dead we discussed in Chapter Two – except that these are rarely family members. Sometimes they belonged to perfect strangers, but have been made 'familiar' through time and attention; in fact, *ñatitas* is a term of affection, it means 'the little pug-nosed ones'. Koudounaris's response to them, I think, is instructive. 'For us,' he explains, 'death is an impassable barricade, but what goes on in Bolivia can only happen when death is a kind of soft barrier, allowing an interaction beyond the divide.' The only thing he found truly surprising was finding something like the custom of *ñatitas* still 'so active in the modern world'.

We are all limited, to an extent, by our own perspectives. This book is written from a largely Western viewpoint, one that accords with experiences in Europe and the US even as it seeks to look beyond them. The lens of culture is useful in breaking down this 'hard' barrier and replacing it with 'soft' ones – but so is the lens of history. The contemporary skulls of Bolivia are not far removed from the decorated seventeenth-century Catholic skeletons (at least on the surface), and some of the practices that may now seem not of this world were nonetheless ingrained in our collective past. This chapter will turn from the 'far away' to the 'long ago', journeying through time instead of space. What we find in the far-flung centuries of Europe or the early days of the US may look, at first, as alien as any sky burial. Welcome to the past, and all its distant dust and daylight.

And for a time, it was 'good'

The Good Death: it's not a phrase that has much currency, today. It does not, specifically, imply a happy end – it may not even refer to an 'easy' passing. It has to do with comportment, our behaviour in the face of death and our preparations for it. The idea of the 'good death', of dying well, is not something that happens to you, it is something you *do*, an active engagement with something that otherwise appears to be a passive and inevitable occurrence.

Social historians remark upon the emergence of this idea, which has been around since at least the eighth century, and probably longer. Philippe Ariès, author of *The Hour of Death*, calls this 'tame' death. Speaking mainly of Europe, he explains that a 'good death' meant the dying had the liberty and presence of mind to set their physical, material and spiritual affairs in order – unlike in earlier times, particularly in our hunter-gatherer past, where death happened suddenly and often violently. As we have already discussed, death can be both event and process, and in these early societies death occurred first and the other-worldly journey happened after death. The idea of a journey hasn't passed away, as proven by practices described in Chapter Two (such as the Tibetan concept of death and rebirth). It has, however, reversed its trajectory in the more recent European past. When hunter-gatherers set up farms, they began the pastoral age and lived more settled lives closer together. They had opportunity and time to plan, and the cycle of the seasons provided a good model for understanding life and death as process *before* the 'event' of death occurred. A cyclical, stationary and mostly unadventurous life provided time to anticipate death and, eventually, to prepare for it. And this changed one thing more: death-as-process became something the dying could participate in *with* the living who remained – not just something that happened after they were gone.

What did a 'good death' entail? Responsibility, for one thing. People now had goods, lands and allegiances to hand down. These social responsibilities were linked to moral expectations. Self-preparation included spiritual preparation, but rather than girding oneself for a journey or battle, the dying were encouraged towards piety and reflection on the life well lived (and the possibility of just deserts). It is not possible – and not very wise – to generalise what that meant for every culture and every time period from antiquity. It's not advisable to make that leap even when limiting the scope to European history. Even so, the concept of *death* as potentially *good* emerges across the West and is the ancestral inheritance of modern Europe and the US. So does it still exist today?

In a 2014 article titled 'Experiencing a Good Death', Susan Spencer writes: 'If you can have a quiet death, or a death with your loved ones around you, then it can really be peaceful and beautiful and meaningful.' Her article describes the death of John Hawkins, a seventy-eight-year-old New York psychotherapist, whose dying was 'chronicled' at home by a photographer.

Hawkins died at home, in hospice care, rather than at the hospital because the clinical setting, suggests Spencer, robs us of the ability to reflect. Dr Jessica Zitter, an ICU (intensive care unit) doctor, comments: 'There's always something physiologically that we can tweak with our ventilators, with our dialysis machines, with our blood pressure support medications. We can always keep *doing things*' [emphasis added]. By foregoing the hospital, Hawkins spent more time with family, wrote his memoir and met regularly with a photographer who would keep a visual record of his dying. If that seems unusual, it should. In the US, only one in four people die at home, though polls suggest more than 70 per cent would like to. According to one BBC report, 60 per cent of British citizens want to die at home, and only 18 per cent manage to. The results are similar in other Western and European countries – doctors are trained to prolong life above all else – well and good, since we want them to protect us from an early end. But as the decorated skeletons photographed by Koudounaris attest, death has an honoured and celebratory place in Western history. Do we still place importance on the idea of dying 'well', or has the idea of a good death simply dropped out of our collective consciousness? This chapter will turn the lens around and look back 'through a glass, darkly' at some key moments in European and US history. From disastrous epidemics to 'natural death', from political upheavals to the professionalisation of the Enlightenment, major events have shaped our approach to mortality in the West.

Danse Macabre: Black Death and rebirth

H istory unspools like an unruly cloth. It snags here, gathers there and frequently takes no settled shape. To get a broader perspective, we necessarily risk losing fine detail. We will start, therefore, with the most famous of mass deaths in European history – the Black Plague. While certainly not the earliest of mortal catastrophes, eruptions of plague in the 1300s and 1400s focused an entire population on the coming end. John Kelly, author of *The Great Mortality*, calls the plague 'apocalyptic' in scale – and so it was. It destroyed lives throughout Europe and parts of Asia, claiming a third of the population

The Dance of Death (1493) by Michael Wolgemut.

(and sometimes more). An astonishing 600 people died a day in parts of France during the worst of it – so many that bodies were sometimes stacked in houses if the mass graves were full or not available. But worse than the sheer numbers of dead and dying (and the horrific stench that this would have caused) was the fact that no one really knew why it was happening or where it was coming from.

One of the greatest tales of the plague's spread has achieved almost mythological status. The year was 1347. Something terrible had arrived at the docks of Genoa, an Italian trading port – something that would change history: ghost ships. The merchant vessels, still laden with their cargo, were also filled with the bodies of putrefying dead men – and those still living didn't look much better, covered as they were with boils that oozed pus and blood. The stench of those closed hulls must have been overpowering, and the authorities refused to let the men or their cargo disembark – but it was too late. For one thing, the bacillus (called Yersina pestis) travelled pneumonically, or through the air, as well as through the bites of rat fleas. For another, no one told the rats, which disembarked down ropes, bringing the pestilence with them. In only a year's time the plague had spread, striking Paris, London and beyond.

The image of the death ship has been forever burned into our cultural memory, and it shows up frequently in horror fiction (the ghost ship *Demeter* in *Dracula,* for instance). But in truth, the merchant ship was only the last link in a long chain of events. Kelly suggests that, from 1250 on, changes in the way people travelled, what and with whom they traded, and environmental/ecological events created a world ripe for disaster. Plagues had been isolated events, but ships, caravans and increasingly crowded cities meant that disease was mobile and could access many more targets. Volcanic eruptions, floods and earthquakes occurred throughout the period, suggesting that the environment was anything but stable – and these events would have changed the weather, sometimes drastically. An Icelandic eruption created an atmosphere thick with particulate: a pale and sickly sky watched over by a cold and distant sun. Even these, however, would not be enough to create the pandemic that levelled Eurasia. Something more was necessary – something like violence and filth and general poor health. The margin between life and death was increasingly narrow in the urban centres of the middle ages. In other words, death did not *arrive* with the plague; it was already *there*.

Life was already hard, and frequently short, in the century before the plague took hold. Nonetheless, death was seen as part of the life cycle and governed by religious understanding. Priests oversaw all funerals and the last rites that preceded them; so important was the Church in the thirteenth century that many auxiliary chapels had to be erected to provide adequate prayer, devotion and funeral practices. Despite difficulties, the death of a child or young person was still considered an event out of the usual order of things, and most lived their lives in pursuit of the 'good death', one that allowed for some preparation. By the fourteenth century, however, the press of the population in urban centres, with too many needs and too few goods, helped to set the stage for something truly terrifying.

What would it mean to live in the squalour of the

pre-plague city? Few practised personal hygiene, as bathing was considered unhealthy. A man or woman might bathe only once or twice a year, and the heavy layers of clothing that guarded against the suddenly cold and unpredictable weather housed all kinds of pestilence, insects, bacteria and mould (a contemporary account describes pests leaping from a disrobed body like the overflow of a fountain). Germ theory was still many centuries away, and superstition largely took the place of medicine. Streets were pitched towards the centre in London so that they served as sewer as well as thoroughfare, crusted with filth and rats and refuse. People typically lived short lives full of suffering, and death — be it animal or human — was everywhere to be seen. Onto this well-prepared stage walked the Black Death in three guises: bubonic (with enormous boils), pneumonic (causing waste of the lungs) and septicemic (which poisoned the blood). Today's apocalyptic narratives of burned-out urban centres populated by walking corpses are not far off the mark.

To know mortality is near is one thing. To know that death stalks the streets and strikes without warning is something else altogether. It makes the 'good death' almost impossible to practice, for that requires time and reflection, and septicemic plague could kill a victim within hours. As death tolls mounted, the thin line of humanity became strained to snapping point. Artwork from the period depicts the dance of death, or *danse macabre*, a gleeful parade of skeletons as they steal life from helpless victims. The ill were boarded up in their homes and the dead buried together in massive graves. The soil of these boneyards became so caustic with bacteria that bodies decomposed to bones with extraordinary rapidity. Finally, with the stench of decay all around and no means of protection, people turned on one another, and innocents (many of them Jews, who were blamed for the plague) were murdered as scapegoats.

Where death reigns, both life and death begin to lose their meaning. In 1348, Giovanni Boccaccio wrote his own eyewitness account of the plague of Florence, explaining that 'as our city sunk into this affliction and misery, the reverend authority of the law, both divine and human, sunk with it' and all became indifferent. Rituals were no longer performed, holy ground was not plentiful enough and bodies littered roadsides and ditches. The dead were no longer 'honoured with tears, lights or companions. Things sunk to the level that people were disposed of much as we would now dispose of a dead goat.' The dead must bury the dead; the living can only flee or wait for the inevitable. And yet, two-thirds of the population did survive. Their attempts to grapple with the immensity of loss remains at the heart of Western tradition – and the Western approach to death was remade and reborn through it. The Black Death may not be the start of European history, but in terms of death-preparation, it was the 're-start'. Nothing would ever be the same.

John Kelly calls the plague era the 'Great Mortality', a time of 'unremitting death' from which Europe emerged 'cleansed and renewed'. But consider: the ubiquity of death had enormous influence on perceptions of death, as well. The rituals of prayers and wakes for the dead had all but been obliterated at the worst of it; in addition, the (largely Christian, largely Catholic) religious systems had broken down and seeds of doubt about sovereignty had been sown. Many priests died, and those that survived often refused to visit the dying and perform last rites. There are tales of great charity during the time of plague, but also of horrific treatment of minority groups (up to and including vicious massacres). Those who lived through the horrors had to come to terms with the enormity of the disaster. The popularity of *Ars Moriendi,* or *The Art of Dying* (Latin texts that advised the reader how to die a good Christian death), in 1415 attests to how heavily mortality weighed on people's minds, but was also revolutionary in its own right: those texts gave people stewardship over death, dying and even last rites, allowing people to perform them without need of the Church. This self-stewardship over life's final moments, which would have been unthinkable before the Black Death, marks one of the first major shifts in European grief culture coming out of the middle ages: death traditions began slowly to shift towards individual experience, instead of religious authority.

In Chapter Two, I spoke about the Cambodians and their response to mass deaths during the Pol Pot period. Genocide, from the death camps of World War II to the slaughter of Tutsi in Rwanda or Sudanese in Darfur, does more than take innocent lives. Suffering on that scale shatters the familiar and makes it difficult for the living to cope psychologically. In the fourteenth century it wasn't a single group, but the whole of Europe and parts of Asia that suffered this kind of fracture – there were no clear targets to blame for the horror and nowhere to go for escape or solace. When tragedy and change on such a scale happens in a single generation, it necessarily shakes the idea that traditions are permanent and immutable. Slowly at first, but picking up speed, the spectre of death underwent incredible transformations in the centuries to come.

From plague to politics: Reformation and (un)holy ground

The Black Plague lingered long in the public imagination, and historical evidence suggests that people in the late medieval period (to the fifteenth century) generally feared the worst, assuming that death was at the door even during mild illness. Of course, in this time of primitive medicine, slight disorders could in fact be fatal. This was especially true for those living at any distance from urban centres, and distance could be as problematic for the dead as for the living. 'Corpse Roads' were built to allow peasants from afar to bring their dead to the churchyard, which was consecrated by a bishop to make it 'holy'. These coffin-paths still remain in parts of the Netherlands and the UK. As Allison Meier of *Atlas Obscura* writes, 'No one wanted rotting bodies hauled through their front yards, so the roads were set up on windswept hills and overgrown pastures where no one wanted to go.' Despite the difficulties, many Europeans still hoped to be buried in 'hallowed ground' and with traditional rites (even if, with the help of the *Ars Morendi*, they could have performed some of these themselves).

In Europe's largely Catholic past, the night after a death was spent in prayer over the body to help the soul on its journey, and the burial took place after a Requiem Mass the next day. During the service, a priest would go into the graveyard and draw a cross on the ground. Afterwards, the body would be carried to the place and seven prayers offered along the way. The corpse would be doused with holy water to keep demons away, and bits of incense and charcoal would be thrown into the grave. The corpse would be aligned with its feet towards the east, and shoes were sometimes left on in case Judgement Day necessitated a lot of walking. It was even believed that those approaching death could see 'over the boundary' between worlds; death was a transition, not a conclusion, and those gathered around the dying would sometimes ask them to be a bridge or go-between, bringing petitions to God. This was, of course, much more serious if the dying person were a saint (or soon to be one), as saints could be powerful friends (or enemies). Prayers would continue to be offered on behalf of the departed long after the funeral was at an end.

Catholic funeral feasts were frequently lavish, and wine and food would be provided even at humbler deaths (scaled to cost). Partly, this was to pacify the living. 'Inebriate conviviality', as Ralph Houlbrooke calls it, 'was one way of drawing death's sting.' Like marriages, death services brought the community together in acts of shared emotion that might remind us of the Torajans. When Henry VII died in 1509, his remains were placed in a chariot draped in black velvet and garnished with gold. According to Paul Fritz, Henry had been embalmed, but a lifelike model dressed in his royal robes rested on top of the coffin, wearing the crown and carrying the sceptre. A huge number of servants surrounded it, and 600 torchbearers followed it. The crowd grew when the chariot reached St Paul's for the first mass and sermon, and the following day the body was taken to Westminster, where another procession of mourners awaited. Three masses followed before the interment, along with equal fanfare and the participation of great crowds of witnesses. But it was not to last: many of the practices that had characterised funerals during this period were about to change.

Rumblings of Reformation

The Protestant Reformation is generally dated to 1517, when Martin Luther published his *Ninety-Five Theses* (*Disputatio pro declaratione virtutis indulgentiarum*). In these, Luther attacked practices of the Catholic Church such as selling indulgences, usury and other abuses of power. A number of things contributed to the Reformation, however, including doubts that arose during those devastating plague years and the 'Western Schism' – which was an internal split of the Catholic Church between two competing papal authorities, one in Rome and the other in Avignon. The dawn of the Renaissance, and a refocusing on the individual and on rational thought, meant various authorities were being called into question. In the 1530s, Henry VIII abolished the Catholic Church in England (mostly for political reasons, but also over issues of sovereignty and divorce), setting off generations' worth of back-and-forth repression and violence between Catholics, Protestants and dissenters.

The Reformation as a title does not have the same dark ring as 'Black Death', but it was an equally painful time of great mortality. This time, however, man fought against man in the Thirty Years' War from 1618 to 1648. Plague had taken a third of the population in the wider theatre of Europe – and now this religious contest, which was fought primarily in present-day

Germany, though involving much of Europe, killed a quarter of all Germans. In his book *The Thirty Years War*, historian Peter Wilson marks its beginning with murder; defiant Bohemian Protestants threw the Catholic Habsburg emperor's envoys from the castle windows in Prague in 1618 (death by defenestration). The Holy Roman Empire responded with sweeping attacks that would eventually ravage parts of Europe from Spain to Sweden. The war officially came to an end in 1648 with the Peace of Westphalia, which supported as one of its tenets the Peace of Augsburg of 1555, meaning princes and principalities had a right to determine which religion would be practised and (in theory) other denominations would be allowed to practise their faith as well. As with all peace treaties, the aims were far too optimistic, but the precedent was enormously important. It meant that the Reformation emphasis on choice and change had won a decisive victory in not only influencing how people worshipped, but also how they lived and how they died. This could not fail to change how they grieved, as well.

The Protestant Reformation was not a single, concerted effort, but the contiguous rise of Lutheran, Calvinist and diversified Reformed churches that broke from Catholic tradition and doctrine. Reformer denominations appeared all over continental Europe, England and Scotland, and the movement dampened certain celebrations that had been linked to Catholic traditions, especially in terms of food and drink (and the impiety caused by all that inebriate conviviality). But the shift away from Catholicism also meant a growing mistrust of certain rituals and ceremonies, as well as the denial of purgatory and the power of prayers for the dead. In countries where

Protestantism gained ground, this effectively severed the tie people had once felt towards the departed, shutting the door between life and death more securely than before. Burial in 'hallowed ground' – so important to death customs – was suddenly considered 'superstitious', while petitions for or to the dead were denigrated as useless. Reformation changes gave more initiative and control to the dying and their families, but, as Houlbrooke reminds us, this came with new challenges – both in terms of cost and of psychological grappling with death itself. If the dead could not be memorialised in the old ways, through close connection and prayer, through the lighted candle, symbolism and religious signs, how were they to be remembered at all?

Leaving the churchyard for the cemetery

I want to return for a moment to the decorated skeletons photographed by Paul Koudounaris. As I mentioned before, they were created as a Catholic response to the Reformation attack on relics. According to Koudounaris, they became popular in the primarily German-speaking areas that the Church hoped to hold onto or even regain from the Protestants. The bones themselves came from Roman catacombs discovered in 1578, but the skeletons were not 'decorated' and venerated until the seventeenth century. At that time, the remains – and Koudounaris suggests there are at least a thousand full or partial skeletons – were authenticated by 'dubious means' as Early Christian martyrs, which gave them a status equivalent to sainthood.

Why so many bones? And why treated in this way? For over a millennia the blessed dead had stood, for Catholic believers, at the side of God, gaining his favour and in turn having the ability to pass that favour on to the living. Koudounaris likens the veneration of bones and skulls of famous Christians to a 'safe version of necromancy', allowing believers to tap into supernatural powers from beyond the grave. In this way, the blessed dead were part of the fabric of life in the Catholic world, with the power to 'assist' the living from beyond. It was this practice, and the power it seemingly gave the Catholic Church, that Protestant reformers sought to do away with. But the bejewelled skeletons remain, their survival a striking reminder that no long-held tradition gives way without a fight.

Turning skeletons into martyrs required labour. The decoration was typically done by teams of nuns north of the Alps; the bones were lined with jewels set in gold filigree wire. In some cases, even wigs were added and the remains dressed in expensive clothing donated by local nobles, which was specially tailored to reveal rather than conceal the bones beneath. In many ways, these skeletal saints received treatment once reserved only for royal funerals, complete with the occasional effigy in wax and painted eyes over the facial bones. They had been reclaimed from the nameless tombs as martyrs in order to reaffirm a Catholic Church on the verge of losing its hold on believers, but in the end, it was a largely futile attempt. Death had begun to take on new meanings in the now-Protestant countries, though, to be fair, it wasn't always in line with official Protestant doctrine.

Reformation teachings about the writing of wills, which frequently stipulated aspects of burial, were generally well received across Europe. However, the desire to venerate the dead was not extinguished, and in fact was probably *strengthened* by prohibitions on praying for the immortal soul. By the late 1600s and early 1700s, emphasis shifted strangely from the spiritual aspects of death (the departed soul) to the physical or material aspects of death (the body and where it lies). For many centuries, and even into the Enlightenment period, bodies were buried in shrouds. Some graves had no markers, and those that did were frequently not made to last. After all, bones could *move* – could be taken up and put into charnel houses – for much of the preceding era. As the dawn of the eighteenth century approached, however, wooden coffins began to become popular, along with 'deep' burial. Rev. Henry Newcombe claims in 1654 to have buried his father-in-law 'deeper than ordinary' to protect the bones from being dug up again or removed, and the addition of grave slabs and other markers may have had similar aims. Monuments and markers also became more popular, while the iconic imagery of intercessory prayer (the dead interceding for the living or the living for the dead) remained, even though, technically speaking, those who commissioned the monuments no longer believed in its power. It is another example of ritual remaining after its meaning had changed. The imagery and the symbol retain importance to mourners as a means of communion with the dead and with each other, and may explain why other types of funerary 'commemoration' increased in significance. Without the original Catholic under-pinnings, however, Protestant nations – and England in particular – struggled to put more spiritual death rituals into practice. Despite some exceptions, death in Protestant countries had begun the slow march towards less supernatural traditions. With the arrival of the Enlightenment in the eighteenth century, illness no longer appeared in the guise of demons and spirits. Instead new discoveries led to disease being seen in a more objective light and even life-threatening illnesses became the purview not of the clergy, but of medicine.

Enlightenment, death and the doctor

Broadly, death in the seventeenth century remained outside the medical jurisdiction, but medical and legal professionals were increasingly part of deathbed deliberations. Physicians had a limited number of resources, not that this kept them from making their best efforts. Granted, these efforts often did as much harm as good. Leslie A. Clarkson cites this account of the Earl of Salisbury in 1612, whose wealth and power were useless in the purchase of 'a peaceful end': 'With swollen legs and a body covered in sores, he was carried on pillows of down in a specially prepared litter from London to Bath whence, it was hoped, the waters might do some good. By now his chaplain was in attendance, for it was clear that the physicians had done their worst.'

One problem that persisted was reliance upon Galen, a Greek physician of the Roman Empire. Though centuries out of date, his understanding of the body and its functions continued to be revered, even though Galen had never dissected a human being in his life. Medicine also relied on the humoral theory, which stated that the body was made up of four 'humours': blood, black bile, yellow bile and phlegm. According to humoral medicine, health was achieved through the balance of these substances – and one way of restoring that balance was to bleed patients (for almost anything). Some advances were made – such as quinine for fever and some surgeries – the success of which contributed to a greater sense of the physician's utility. With the arrival of Enlightenment ideals, death became subject to rational investigation.

The Age of Enlightenment, also called the Age of Reason, encompassed most of the eighteenth century and marked a shift in Western philosophy, beginning with the works of John Locke. Locke's *Two Treatises of Government* (1690) established a revolutionary rhetoric that hailed political 'subversion' (or revolt) on the grounds of reason and individualism. Locke questioned the basis for kingly authority; he then proposed a 'rights-based' justice that set limits on those in power. He viewed certain revolutions (like England's 'Glorious Revolution' of 1688, when subjects overthrew James II in favour of Parliamentarians and William of Orange) as a reasonable step taken by reasonable men. Reason becomes more important than authority and supplants the 'law of God'. This would ultimately have implications for death customs.

Enlightenment ideology developed almost simultaneously in France, Britain, Germany, the Netherlands, Italy, Spain, Portugal and the American colonies. It influenced revolutions:

the authors of the American Declaration of Independence, the United States Bill of Rights, the French Declaration of the Rights of Man and others were motivated by its principles. At its core, the Enlightenment shared with the Reformation a focus on individual experience and a willingness to question authority – even the authority of death. It also supported scientific enquiry and the 'scientific revolution', privileging empirical, evidence-based knowledge over traditional understanding and opening a doorway to medicine.

Before the Age of Enlightenment, Christian ideology generally portrayed death (for the unrepentant) as the 'Terror of Terrors' and the wages of sin. Historian of medicine Roy Porter explains that within that paradigm, medical procedures 'remained in the shadows, secondary, almost irrelevant', because death was the province of God. With the arrival of Enlightenment thought, however, came doubts about the afterlife, and the philosopher David Hume suggested that oblivion was all that awaited the dying (no endless bliss or punishment).

But this alone did not make death an enemy. Famed surgeon John Hunter's dying words in 1793 reflect this: 'If I had a pen in my hand now, and were able to write, I could tell how easy and pleasant a thing it is to die.' That does not mean people went quietly to their graves, however. In fact, social critic Ivan Illich suggests that it was from the Enlightenment period that doctors began to feel they had a right, and even the ability, to conquer death. Roy Porter questions the universal nature of that view, but medical care at the deathbed had certainly become a hallmark of eighteenth-century living and dying, as medicine became primarily interested in prolonging life. Philosophers even began to speculate on the possibility of immortality on earth, the conquest of death and disease, and the denial of death. When it occurred, death had new scientific names: fever, scurvy, influenza, pulmonary infection, smallpox, typhoid and various other conditions. More importantly, death began to be perceived as an untimely event and the middle class employed doctors (and their methods) to hold death at bay. In the end, however, death would still come.

In this period, fear of death remained central. According to John McManners, author of *Death and the Enlightenment*, only 200 of every 1,000 babies born in France would live to the age of fifty. At the same time, the eighteenth century saw a growing individualism, even to the point of turning away from religion. The individual was fast becoming more important – and so the individual's life, be they king or pauper, became increasingly worth preserving. This new importance of self, coupled with the Enlightenment shift towards the rational, meant the threat of oblivion was possibly *more* terrifying than the old Catholic understanding of hellfire. The Enlightenment's gifts were decidedly two-edged.

Enlightenment science rendered doctors more important, even if they were not necessarily more competent in the face of mortality. Even so, great strides had been made in medicine: quinine (as mentioned earlier), smallpox inoculations, better understanding of anatomy (including the anatomy of pregnant women), the prevention of scurvy with citrus, the first success-ful appendectomy (1736 – Claudius Aymand) and the discovery of nitrous oxide's anaesthetic properties (1799). A growing interest in electricity ended in some very strange attempts to reanimate dead tissue, most notably the public demonstration by Galvani's nephew Giovanni Aldini, who used electric pulses on dead Newgate criminals. (The experiment caused arms and legs to twitch and jump, and likely influenced Mary Shelley's *Frankenstein*.) But what influence did this new science have on the way people looked after and mourned their dead? Roy Porter acknowledges the influence of doctors in changing the 'face of death', but explains that they did so *not* by subduing it or reducing how often it occurred. Instead, they helped to shift the public perception of it as something to be fought and conquered. More importantly for us, as inheritors of these earlier traditions, doctors became more expected at deathbeds and more authoritative about death and its process.

The four-century lesson

What, then, can four centuries teach us about Western philosophies of death? To begin, the Black Death encouraged people to contemplate life's fleeting nature. The pious would gaze upon wax effigies of rotting corpses (strange, considering how many actual corpses were likely to have been around). Skulls and crossbones and paintings of death appeared everywhere. The wealthy even paid to use that caustic, bacteria-laden soil from mass burials in their own vaults or coffins, as the ability to quickly reduce the body to a skeleton became fashionable. Such things speak to a culture so immersed in death that its very ubiquity takes away from the sting. When grave-dirt becomes a commodity, taken from mass graves and put inside the coffins of well-to-do dead, we know that death is king. Contemplation of mortality did not end with the plague, but it certainly changed, shape-shifting through the Reformation and the Enlightenment until it arrived at a strange state of contradiction. In the centuries to follow, despite an increase in death commodities, death itself would become a bitter pill to swallow, frequently seeming an 'unnatural' or 'untimely' end.

It is, however, too simplistic to say that as religious structures waned, burgeoning secularisation encouraged people to deny and perhaps to try conquering death. The Reformation and Enlightenment periods were not atheistic ones; if anything, religious sentiment polarised between the Catholics and Protestants – while Dissenters and non-Christians continued to struggle for the right to live and die according to their beliefs. Science and medicine had begun their slow march against mortality, but death remained very much a part of life in ways that may seem closer to the customs of the Torajans, Tibetans and Cambodians than to present-day practices in Europe and the US. The years that followed the plague saw the slow shift from a centralised religious authority over death, one that kept supernatural ties to the dead open and potentially powerful, to a more individualised understanding of death, dying and grieving – but one that privileged the 'rational' over the 'spiritual'. By the eighteenth century, the dawn of Enlightenment science changed approaches to death once more. And by looking specifically at the eighteenth-century funeral in France and England, we begin to see something that resembles our modern age. We begin, that is, to see something of our own reflection.

In eighteenth-century France, when someone died in a village, a message would be sent to the bell-ringer. The change ringing that followed would give the age and sex of the deceased, so that you truly knew 'for whom the bell tolled'. Prayers would be said, the eyes of the dead closed and then women would take care of the body. Once cleaned and wrapped in a shroud, the corpse would be surrounded by candles and (for those still residing in largely Catholic nations like France) holy water for sprinkling. Clocks in the house would be stopped at the hour of death, mirrors turned to the wall and beehives cloaked in black fabric. In England, too, 'telling the bees' of a death was commonly practised, and it was feared that forgetting to do so would result in the bees leaving the hive. Change ringing also persisted in rural England into the twentieth century. In both France and England, death was the scene of communal gathering; songs would be sung, stories told. The Catholic clergy were actively discouraged from giving sermons, but sermons became the expected procedure in Protestant countries such as England – although both the pious and the Enlightenment rationalists of the eighteenth century agreed that a funeral should be conducted with solemnity, restraint and simplicity.

Interestingly, the piety of the deceased began to matter less and less; the 'good death' had changed. One might still aim for careful preparation before death – especially those with wealth to distribute – but the spiritual element had become more about procedure than faith practice. Even in France, only the excommunicates, Jews and active Protestants were denied interment even in 'holy' ground. The dead might, however, skip interment altogether – they certainly did so in England, where it was not unheard of to offer one's corpse to science for dissection. Even those who were interred might not stay that way, as burial did not inhibit the 'resurrection men' who dug up bodies for profit (something I will return to in Chapter Five). In France, such practices were much more rare, but the simple funeral became the height of good taste – not only for the humble or pious, but as a more secular convention.

The funeral was a space of enormous political potential and symbolism in the eighteenth century (which followed hard after bloody revolutions in Germany and England, and saw additional revolutions in the American colonies and in France). In Germany, thanks in part to the Thirty Years' War, the Reformation set the standard for funerals, redefining religious dogma and also allowing the state to play a much larger role. Martin Luther sought to reduce the symbolic power of the clergy, and the celebration of the departed was transformed into a lesson for the living. But society, like nature, abhors a vacuum and symbolism was taken up once more – this time by persons, principalities and political power struggles. In eighteenth-century German funerals, a master of ceremonies was often employed; the *Sorgemann* was the chief mourner and determined who might be invited into the house. Mourning could still be symbolic, but the symbols increasingly became markers of economic wealth, nationalism and patriotism – best illustrated by two eighteenth-century examples: firstly the death of German bookseller Gottfried Schultze, and secondly, the French national monument designed by Jean-Baptiste Pigalle (as recounted by John McManners in *Death and the Enlightenment*).

Schultze was very well-to-do. His brother acted as his chief mourner, and personal invitations were sent to prominent figures. Two pairs of Doctors at Law and two of medicine were invited as 'friends of the house', though from the record McManners gives, there were ultimately four of each. The main mourners followed the corpse, with twenty each of doctors and preachers, ten senators in total and thirty-two licentiates (or persons with a degree). A procession of people followed behind, forming a line so long that when the Sorgemann entered the church, it stretched far behind and outside. One hundred and twenty-one people wore long mourning cloaks and thirty wore short ones, and though the service itself was simple, the whole funeral made a lasting impression about who Schultze was and why he mattered.

The monument of Marshall Saxe, crafted by Pigalle, was completed in 1777. Like the British tomb of Lord Nelson, this artful grave embodies what David Irwin considers contemporary attitudes to death, and the sculpted pieces use symbolism once reserved for the clergy. Saxe, celebrated for his military victories, died in 1750. Pigalle's original design included the figure of France, as a woman, weeping over the marshall. The design selected by the king, however, shows a 'proud and confident Saxe', still in command and marching with purpose towards an open coffin, flags to the right and the lion, leopard and eagle to the left. France's military power is further secured, explains Irwin, by the figure of Hercules, a pagan holdover from mythology and rather an odd fit for a church monument. The entirety of the tomb is a parable, a literary representation and allegory that serves to aggrandise the state and secure allegiance. The fanfare, the spectacle, the commual nature of celebration flies in the face of the *danse macabre* tradition.

What can we learn from the funeral and subsequent memorials to Schultze and Saxe? Though elements of medieval funerals can still be seen, such as candles and even some of the liturgy, the primary emphasis here is upon life. Schultze's funeral told onlookers something about the man and his accomplishments, even though he was neither a royal, a statesman or a general. Saxe's monument likewise tells a story, this time a national one, about accomplishment (and so not to be described through weeping women). In general, eighteenth-century funerals were not meant as a lesson about mortality, and those who attended were not called upon to reflect in turn on their own deaths the way their medieval ancestors had been. That did not make everyone happy; theologians complained of it from the pulpit, as did lawmakers. McManners points to an eighteenth-century lawyer who lamented that the death penalty itself had become pointless as a teaching tool. No one paid the lesson any mind. In fact, by the 1790s, few wished to think or speak of death. Avert your eyes, do not see and, whenever possible, use a syllogism. And yet, in the midst of this contradictory familiarity and denial of mortality, something new arose: a commodity culture of death. What the eighteenth-century citizen *spent* upon the funeral becomes significant.

Author Mike Rendell has recorded the funeral arrangements for the wife of his British ancestor, Richard Hall. In 1780, the funeral accoutrements included coffin lining and mattress, lead coffin and plate inscription, an elm case with cherubim handles, candlesticks, death notices, funds for draping his shop and home in mourning, a large number of laced gloves and other smaller items. The final tally, according to Rendell, was about £51 (£3,500 today) – and these items all had to come from somewhere, from shops and boutiques that existed for the purpose of supplying the *objects* of mourning, the *things* of death. The cost of funerals and the associated expectations – the keeping up of appearances – only grows as we move from the eighteenth to the nineteenth century. Supported by the commodity culture that emerged from the industrial revolution, and made possible by new technologies like photography, the boundary between living and dead, person and thing, becomes very 'soft' indeed. And through the Victorians – in so many ways our near ancestors – we may begin to see how science begins to assume its active role not only in death, but also in shaping our approach to grief.

Chapter 4

DYING VICTORIAN: MEMENTO MORI, HAIR JEWELLERY AND CRAPE

The complex death culture
of the nineteenth century

It is a peaceful image. A woman, sitting in a rocking chair, gazes reflectively into the foreground. Behind her is the patterned wallpaper that graced the parlours of many a Victorian home. Her head rests upon lace, possibly her own handiwork, and nearby is a shelf of small vials, the homemaker's apothecary. Graceful, quiet, restful.

There is only one problem: this woman is dead.

Example of a Victorian memento mori photograph.

It is remarkable how hard the photographer worked to make the picture appear natural and the corpse a living being. Why go to so much trouble? Only decades before, the body would have been wrapped and laid in a churchyard, dirt scattered directly on top of the remains. In the nineteenth century, however, a sudden vigorous interest in coffins and in public cemeteries arose, and with it a peculiarly popular craze: permanently memorialising and displaying the dead (or parts of them). In this chapter, we will look at the complex mourning rituals of Victorian culture, from jewellery made of the deceased's hair to photographic memento mori.

In late medieval era Catholic monasteries, the devout would sometimes contemplate a symbolic wax representation of a dead body to remind them of their own mortality and that they should not be attached to worldly things, but instead focus their attention on the spiritual. This practice was not exclusive to Christians, however; Buddhist monks were also encouraged to consider the slow rot of (usually female) corpses. These depicted the nine stages of decay and were represented on painted scrolls called *kusôzu*. The British Museum has a fine example (see page 102), a painted scroll depicting the body of a women (a courtesan) slowly rotting, being torn apart by dogs and ultimately dispersed. It was meant to disturb and sicken the viewer, who observed a beautiful female body as it became bloated, discoloured, horrible and – as a result – undesirable. This version is from the 1870s (contemporary to the Victorians), but the practice goes back to much more ancient traditions – reminiscent of the *danse macabre*.

The kusôzu served a dual purpose: to remind the watcher

The kusôzu (1870s), British Museum.

of their own impending death, but also to encourage chastity. A courtesan was a woman of pleasure or a prostitute, and this was a way of saying 'beneath her beauty lie but bones'. Exactly how effective this was is hard to guess. In ancient Egypt, for instance, death was not considered enough of a sexual deterrent for royal embalmers. In the event of a princess dying they were not per-mitted to begin embalming for at least three days, to make it less likely that they would fornicate with her corpse. There is an obviously gendered element to these early considerations, with women's bodies often the focus of anxiety; even in death, it seems, women have historically been viewed as objects.

As discussed in Chapter Three, objects of morbid fascina-tion – such as pendants of gold shaped like skeletons, skull rings and memento mori – became popular among the wider population, and by the eighteenth century they were com-modities, rendered ornate, made of gold and transformed into pendants and brooches. On one hand, such items were meant to represent the transience of material luxury. On the other hand, the fact that they were made of precious metals appears to be at odds with their purpose. Material goods pass away,

A gold pendant, an example of Victorian mourning jewellery.

but the symbols of that passage were beautified. Why? Were they intended to be memorials to the dead? Or do they speak to the way that 'grave' goods can become fashionable? This is an especially appropriate question when we look at Victorian mourning, which supported an entire grief industry. By means of clothing, jewellery and photographs, grief could be displayed among mourners, clothiers, tailors, artisans and curious viewers of the funeral parade.

A short history of shifting death culture

The Victorian death culture arose out of a confluence of events – and major social and cultural changes. Heir to the Enlightenment, the Victorian age – from roughly 1837 until 1903 – was a time of industrialism, science, rationality and *transformation*. The seventeenth century saw the English Civil War, much unrest and a number of plague outbreaks; the eighteenth century, though known as the Age of Enlightenment, was in some respects rather like a loud and bawdy bar-room brawl that lasted more than a hundred years. The middle class began to form during this same period, evolving partly from the merchants who had raised themselves through labour to a higher station than their parents and grandparents. By the middle and latter eighteenth century this new class, which valued sober living and hard work, was attempting to impose a strong work ethic and moral instruction on not only the desperate and rough-living poor below them, but the decadent and over-indulged aristocrats *above* them as well. Unsurprisingly, this was a slow process, and society continued to divide itself between haves and have-nots – a situation reflected in some unusual death practices. For instance, it was once a custom in England to pay poor people to 'take on the sins' of the wealthy dead. This is sometimes referred to as the practice of *sin-eating*, and while it has lately become the stuff of film scripts, it was a genuine death custom:

> 'When the corpse was brought out of the house and laid on the bier, a loaf of bread was brought out, and delivered to the sin-eater over the corpse, as also a [. . .] bowl full of beer, which he was to drink up [. . .] whereof he took upon him [. . .] all the sins.'

The 'improper' behaviour of a rich person was therefore erased (in theory) – which rendered the religious aspect of funerals rather irrelevant.

Even so, such practices were fading with the Enlightenment,

replaced by rationalism, science and medicine – and a new professional class that sought to practise them. Dissection and anatomy changed everything from the treatment of disease to the birthing of babies. That isn't to suggest that superstitious rituals vanished entirely – but they did evolve. The new interest in coffins and heavy-duty lids might not have been rooted in dread of the undead, but a consequence of anatomy itself; after all, the bodies had to come from somewhere, refrigeration was not possible and embalming was still some decades off. Even the 'hallowed ground' of the churchyard did not keep out the body-snatchers, who continued to sell cadavers to anatomy students.

Despite such dirty dealings and despite Enlightenment sentiments, churchyards were still full – full to bursting – of the decaying dead. Tiny church properties were not adequate to contain the newly dead of London's exploding population; St Martin-in-the-Fields, which was only about 200 feet square, contained almost 70,000 bodies. The consequence of over-burying is still felt today – in August of 2013, the BBC reported that Bath Cathedral might collapse because its floor was built on top of 6,000 shallow graves.

Why so crowded? It wasn't all piety. Churchyards were not picky about who you were; anyone could be buried there and it wasn't expensive (or didn't have to be). Mainly the expense came from the funeral preparation and certain payments to the Church authorities, but if all you needed was a hole in the ground, little else was required. Opulent funerals were available only to the wealthy, but in churchyards people of all classes were buried together – and the living, rich and poor, found themselves crammed into tiny churchyards to mourn in uncomfortable proximity. Considering the long shadow cast by the plague years, no one of 'substance' wanted to be near possible sources of contagion. It wasn't long before those with money and means went looking for other places to inter their dead.

In an increasingly global and digital world, the keeping of strict social hierarchies can sometimes seem out of step with modern experience. It remains, however, deeply entrenched, in ways both subtle and more obvious. The gap between the 'haves' and 'have-nots' has never disappeared, of course, but in the Victorian period it was far more visible. In Britain, small children worked in factories, or walked barefoot through the muck of the Thames to find nails to sell, or swept filthy streets for pennies. Journalist Henry Mayhew published a series in the 1840s called *London Labour and the London Poor*, and much of what he related there influenced the novels of Charles Dickens. When you read about Tiny Tim in *A Christmas Carol*, or about Poor Joe in *Bleak House*, you aren't getting sensationalism – you are seeing things as they often really were. Life was dirty, dark and hard for the poor in Victorian London, and the difference between rich and poor extended right down to the way you died and how you were buried.

The beautiful (dead) people

Britain's first major public cemeteries (as distinct from churchyards) opened in the early nineteenth century. Kensal Green, Norwood, Highgate and the Glasgow Necropolis all opened before 1850, and most operated with a sliding fee scale relating to how and where the dead would be interred.

Pause for a moment to consider this: the notion of paying a large sum of money to be buried was almost entirely new. Today, we hardly raise an eyebrow at the thought of pricey plots; they are, in fact, among the most expensive real estate going. Why did the Victorians pay these new fees? The answer isn't simple. First, there was the allure of social superiority: not only would your remains be buried away from the lowly poor, but your relatives wouldn't have to mix with lower-class mourners. What's more, a new 'aesthetic' of death had emerged, one that saw cemeteries as wide open spaces, graceful parks, stately grounds.

Let's look again at the two death announcements in the Introduction to this book (pages 6 and 7), and the difference between 'moulders here' and 'slumbers here'. A euphemism is a bit like talking about what you aren't talking about: it skirts around a subject, but allows us to keep speaking the unspeakable – stripping a taboo subject of 'offensive' overtones. The linguist Eliecer Fernandez has looked at obituaries in the Victorian period and finds similar shifts of language to those on death notice cards. The word 'obituary' is itself a euphemism that means 'departure' in Latin. In the notice on page 7 the image is of a gate, leading to a shining city – the gates are open to receive the 'departing' spirit. Beneath, it reads 'Gone but not forgotten', and 'gone' also suggests taking leave, rather than the obliteration of death. The poem that follows uses more of these departure words: vacant, gone, a place unfilled. The soul has been 'recalled' by God – it is on a spiritual road trip. These writings might suggest that the primary reason for speaking of death in this way was strict adherence to religious practice, but in fact, strict, traditional religious practice was in decline in the Victorian period. Yet the euphemisms persist and proliferate, in part because this language is more beautiful, more poetic. A change was advancing, and it had an artistic purpose as well as a social one. Beauty was becoming part of death.

This necessarily began with the upper classes – people who had the leisure and the money to prepare for this new kind of dying, and of memorialising. Compared to the grim, gothic spaces of earlier burial sites, cemeteries became leafy pleasure grounds, and there was a corresponding desire to render the corpse itself as unchanging, eternal in its beauty.

The Enlightenment-born understanding of individuality contributed to this. The more we understand ourselves and others as unique individuals, the more we see the body as the place where that unique identity resides. Concern with the body's appearance is related to our understanding of who the deceased was in life, which explains the kind of comments you might sometimes hear at funerals in the US, where open caskets are the norm: 'He would *never* wear that shirt.' This practice of preparing a body to be viewed – and to be beautiful – was made popular by the Victorians, who even went to great lengths to make corpses look younger and more beautiful in death than in life. False teeth, false hair, dyed hair, make-up, and clothing produced especially for the funeral were all part of the process. The only trouble was the body's transience. As Sarah Tarlow explains, 'from the eighteenth century we see increasing efforts being made by the bereaved to extend their emotional relationships past the death of a loved one'. Even though the Victorian age was characterised by the rise of rationality, science and a decreased religiosity, the desire for continuance and ritual remained strong – and even grew and solidified. What the Victorians needed, and wanted, was a way to make these relationships more permanent.

The intimacy of 'things'

Relics work as traces of a life and body completed and disappeared, in this sense something like last words, but they also serve as frames or fragments of the moment of loss.

—Deborah Lutz

The Victorian images of death as sleep provided private and eternal snapshots of rest, intended to remain long after bodies had decayed. In this way, clothing, jewellery and photos were all relics, pieces of the person who has died. But some of the most touching images are those of parents cradling a dead child – and these do more than memorialise the dead, they memorialise the grieving and so, too, the grief. Look at the patient, stoic, pained expression of the mother as she hovers over a dead infant and consider: why would this be something you might wish to capture and display? Is this public display of grief appropriate or desirable? The answer, for the Victorians, was *yes*. All grief was public grief. When Queen Victoria's husband Albert died, she wore black 'weeds' for the rest of her life and was, in many respects, defined by her grief. It has

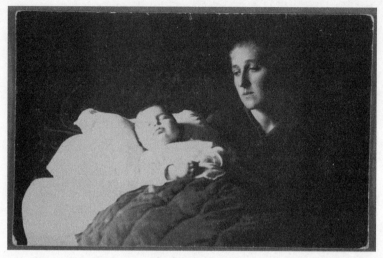

Memento mori photograph showing a mother with her dead child.

been argued that the responsibility for making mourning 'fashionable' lies with her – by the height of the Victorian period, widows were living memorials to their husband's death, and while grieving lasted for shorter periods following the loss of wives or children, it was still always something you displayed to the world.

Queen Victoria's extended mourning ushered in a strict code of fashion. In the first year of mourning a widow wore black crape, a scratchy silk material that was stiff, crimped and reflected no light. In her second year she wore 'secondary mourning', which was still black but might be trimmed with white collars or cuffs. 'Ordinary mourning' was next – again, still black, but now the fabric could be shiny – and then 'half-mourning', when gray or purple was permitted. Men also wore mourning attire, but the fashion of grief seemed particularly engineered for women's wear, and a widow's grieving period was longest of all. Deborah Lutz, a professor and historian of death and mourning, calls these 'secular relics'.

In Western Europe's Catholic past, monasteries and cathedrals housed relics of saints or other holy objects – and many still do. The holiest ones are usually associated with Christ or the Virgin Mary, and might be items they are rumoured to have touched or worn during their lifetimes. Splinters of wood from the 'true cross' are among these – but as historians are quick to point out, if all the splinters given that name were put together you would have a forest, not a cross. It is difficult to tell, without documentation or provenance, where something has come from – but the most common relics are associated with apostles or the saints, or their remains. These, by their nature, are considered holy or sacred relics; a secular relic, by contrast, is an object of deep *personal* meaning to an individual, family or community who knew and cared for the dead. Other cultures also have relics of this sort; as we discussed in Chapter Two, some cultures make their dead part of the family (or at least part of the furniture).

In Victorian Britain, particularly at mid-century, it became increasingly popular to hold on to remains – to linger over a lock of hair or some other testament to the now-dead beloved. Lutz describes the two sides of this trend: that it represented both the desire for the loved one's 'soul' to live on, and a willingness to dwell on the moment of loss, as though death itself was tangible. Relics, in their physical presence, have a kind of narrative power. It is for this reason that they find their way into so much Victorian fiction – often as plot devices that turn the story or reveal a secret – and it is true of the early

Gothic tradition as well. In fact, a memento mori in the form of a decaying figure made of wax appears centre stage in Ann Radcliffe's *The Mysteries of Udolpho*, while a memento miniature picture drives the plot on.

What constituted a secular relic in the Victorian period? It was not, as in Catholic reliquaries, the actual bones and teeth and blood of a dead person. Instead, an inanimate object, sometimes an heirloom, frequently took on specialised meaning. In that sense, people – as bodies – became 'things', and 'things' took on a life of their own. The Victorians were on a trajectory away from supernatural explanations, but a good deal of Victorian science retained other-worldly perspectives. For instance, the séance took on new relevance as a pseudo-science (Arthur Conan Doyle, author of the Sherlock Holmes mysteries, was an avid attendee.) Even stranger, from the 1870s, it was thought that memories could move outside of the human mind and attach themselves to – and even 'haunt' – objects.

This idea developed during the Victorian era from existing concepts of telepathy and ancestral memory, among other things. Objects were thought to collect trauma around them like memory sponges, meaning that trauma itself was transferable and could be passed from one person to the next through a trace of the memory. The idea appears in fiction, like Conan Doyle's 'The Leather Funnel', in which a host asks his guests to sleep in the same room as an ancient torture device. Though the narrator isn't told of the history of the object, he dreams of the horrible execution of a woman. This represents a rather sadistic turn in the host (worst overnight ever), but the popularity of the story also demonstrates how memory-laden objects appealed to a wide audience. Objects told stories, and the inherited possessions of a dead loved one even more so.

Relics like these became a virtual 'craze' from 1850 to 1880, and a trade flourished to take advantage of the new aesthetic of death. Jewellery was perhaps the most popular kind of memento – particularly hair jewellery, such as the mourning pendant. Advertisements for such products appeared in newspapers. One from *Godey's Magazine* provides a range of choices: bracelets, earrings, breastpins, rings, fob chain, charms, studs and sleeve buttons. The *Illustrated London News* carried specialised advertisements for Christmas, suggesting that mourning rings might make excellent seasonal presents. They were elegant, sometimes bejewelled and – like the memento mori pendants of gold – they were more than a statement of death: they were also objects of beauty, status and desire. In a paper entitled 'Sentimental Cuts: Eighteenth-Century Mourning Jewelry with Hair', the art historian Christiane Holm suggests that 'the focus of mourning is no longer the mourned and their fame, but instead the mourners and their mourning.' Of course, it is also about the object itself, the way it carries memory and can display grief to the world (while also looking lovely).

Hair art for the mourner is bound up, in part, with lovelocks (the bits of hair given to a woman's betrothed). In that sense, then, it could potentially mislead as a symbol. However, mourning jewellery was not worn alone. These relics were embellishments on a costume of grief, and the primary function of mourning wear was to *identify* the bereaved. In 1840, Basil Montagu records that 'in the mourning dress, the outward sign of sorrow, we call for the solace of compassion, for

Example of a mourning brooch, containing locks of human hair.

the kind words and looks of friends and for the chastened mirth of strangers, who, unacquainted with the deceased, respect our grief'. In fact, Victorian etiquette manuals told their readers that displaying grief outwardly would soothe them – and would 'protect' women from unwanted advances. It also, of course, supplied an industry.

In 1889, *Good Housekeeping* happily listed the year's latest mourning dress in its column on 'Family Fashions and Fancies'. The column compares English and French styles of crape, and then lists the proper etiquette for the season:

'The dress for mid-summer or mid-winter is Henrietta cloth or bombazine trimmed with deep folds of crape or made with an entire skirt of crape. [. . .] It is becoming the custom to adopt French fashions in lightening the mourning. These are in marked contrast to severe English styles. The French milliners' bonnets are decked in jet and even ostrich tips are used. While these fashions would seem in the worst taste for regular mourning dress, they may be introduced to lighten mourning with excellent effect.'

The article goes on to detail the mourning fashions in New York, a discussion of 'ostentatious' or ill-made mourning dress, and proper accoutrement from caps to greeting cards. Additional accounts can be found in the 1876 *Millinery Trade Review*, a magazine for those in the tailoring trade. Here, the talk is partly about how to make proper wear for different cultures and levels of society – for instance, 'crape flowers', though popular on the continent, are 'not liked by ladies of taste' in the US. Mourning wear even has its own chapter in Richard Well's 1894 edition of *Manners, Culture, and Dress of the Best American Society* – so the Victorian emphasis on grief was shared beyond Britain.

It was also, however, quite expensive and not available to all. A letter quoted in the nineteenth-century literary magazine *Polyanthos* complains that full mourning is 'a hot and expensive dress', and that the cost of a single pair of mourning gloves would keep the correspondent 'in curry and rice for half a year'. Even so, most widows would not – excuse the pun – be caught dead wearing inappropriate mourning dress; not only in service to the departed, but also to avoid being cried down by a watching public.

In many respects, then, while secular relics commemorated the dead, mourning dress was still for the benefit of the living. Expenses could be high – even exorbitant – and this was eventually censured even by the Queen, in 1875. At the same time, mourning dress created a culture where grief for the dead was public; something that, in the US and UK at least, is no longer the case. Yet I imagine many today might find the idea appealing. If you have ever been through personal tragedy, you may well have felt hurt and offended by the world around you, which doesn't slow down or take any notice of your suffering. Haven't you ever longed for a space of even a few days where people – friends and strangers alike – paused respectfully to consider your loss? Today's relentless pace demands that most of us schlep along as before, with little time available to stop and really reflect on, or live with, our grief – ultimately the best way to help us pass through it. The cost and time of making or wearing mourning clothing and mourning jewellery forced a pause, and created space for grief (both private and public). When the mourner was ready to move from black to gray, they were actually performing a rite of passage not unlike the one performed at the abused women's shelter described in Chapter One. Ritual helped the Victorians to express their emotions, as well as giving them a way to move on from one stage to the next.

Memento mori photography

What I always found most compelling was the beauty of the images and that you could find poignant poses and stories to be told in these bizarre (I thought at the time) photographs.

—Steve DeGenero, Collector

So what role, in all of this, do photographs play? The Victorian culture of death was one of memory and nostalgia, taking in concepts of 'displaced' memory – memory that clung to objects – premonitions, 'inherited' memory and more. The sweet sense of the past, mixing with still-circulating ideas about ghosts and séances, elevated fleeting sensations: all things ephemeral are made lovely in their brevity. But at the same time, Victorians sought to capture this ephemeral and fleeting beauty – and, after capturing it, to put it on display.

Memento mori photography is necessarily a late invention; the daguerreotype, which was the first camera technology, arrived in the 1830s. Unfortunately, it was labour-intensive and expensive, involving copper plates fronted in silver, mercury fumes and iodine crystals – and it took a lot of time. As a result, it was out of most people's price range, and remained so even after cheaper materials and production became available. In fact, sometimes the *only* family photo was a post-mortem; too expensive for everyday use, photography would still be cheaper than a portrait painter. And how else would you remember the dead? It is hard to imagine, in our digital age, but for most people in most centuries, all you had was a memory. And this returns us to the original use of memento mori. Literally translated from the Latin, it means 'remember you will die' – it referred to the contemplation of other dead persons as a reminder of your own impending fate. But though photography was a new kind of death-imaging, photographing your dead *as though they were alive* is a denial of death, and another popular Victorian practice, photographing the living *with* the dead, blurs the line between life and death itself.

This lovely daguerreotype image in velvet (see below) comes from the collection of Steve DeGenero; he has several of these, and was kind enough to let me handle them. They are, without doubt, works of art. The daguerreotype process was invented in 1839 in France and came to the US right away; other processes followed in the 1850s. DeGenero explains the daguerreotype as superior to the ambrotype and tintype (on glass and metal plates respectively), though they were more durable, involved less dangerous chemicals and had faster exposure times. I mention the process here because we, with our digital cameras and Instagrams, don't always realise the incredible time and energy that went into these creations. It was not just a matter of staging and having a good eye; photographers were chemists, and their subjects not very different from painters' models.

Like me, you may have seen photos like these before online. Holding the gilt frame in your hands, however, is an entirely new experience. The daguerreotype is heavy. It is made of copper and silver, after all. It has *weight* – a presence – a

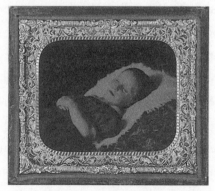

Daguerreotype in velvet.

'thing-ness'. And in cradling it, I was cradling the dead child as well as the final touching moments of someone's hopes and dreams. At the same time, the image doesn't have the kind of *finality* you might expect from a post-mortem. The child appears to be contentedly slumbering, even as the woman in the rocking chair at the start of this chapter appeared to be having a quiet moment of reflection. Even wasting or communicable disease is absent in this beauty rest. DeGenero has an image in his collection of a child posed on a couch, but careful inspection makes it clear that the photo was taken *through a window*. This was not artistic licence. If you look closely, there is a small sign on the window. It reads: 'smallpox quarantine'. As he explains, 'Thinking about how the family and the photographer had to improvise to accomplish the task made the photo even more precious. The family needed a visual reminder – a memento mori – and even infectious disease wouldn't stop them.'

If hair jewellery functions as a relic and mourning dress as a public expression of sorrow, the memento mori photograph provides something more. The camera allows for a make-believe world, a place to pretend the dead are yet living, a space where the living and the dead can both exist together. It freezes time – not as it is, but as you wish it were. Some of my favourite images are of parents and children – or of siblings. Sometimes, it is difficult to tell who in the picture is living and who is dead. The best examples have been collected by Stanley B. Burns; in his impressive archive are numerous examples of sibling pairs wherein one of the pair has died. In many photos, the bodies are propped up, the eyes held open (sometimes paint was applied, if necessary), and the living and dead posed for their picture together. It might be as simple as holding a deceased infant as though it were sleeping (below), or as complex as creating the illusion of two children at play. Complex directions were often given – the photo of a deceased middle-aged man in DeGenero's collection includes pencilled instructions on the back (see pages 121 and 122). Though the scrawl is somewhat difficult to read, it essentially tells the photographer to take the man out of his coffin and then

A mother with her dead child.

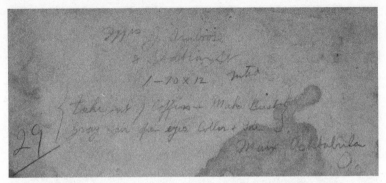

Pencilled instructions on posing the body for the photographer.

explains how to pose him – right down to the way his hair ought to lie around his eyes to make him appear most lifelike. In fact, this desire to imitate nature was part of the advertising campaign for American photographers of the dead: 'Secure the Shadow, Ere the Substance Fade, / Let Nature imitate what Nature made.'

Jay Ruby, author of *Secure the Shadow: Death and Photography in America*, describes the desire for memento mori photography of this kind as a contest between public denial of death and the desire to memorialise the dead – but it also represents a desire for participation. Victorians not only photographed the newly dead, they also used new imaging techniques to bring back the long-dead – a kind of photographic séance.

One of the most famous practitioners of spirit photography was William Mumler. He produced double-exposed photographs, claiming that he was capturing the spirits of the dead (including a photograph of Mary Todd Lincoln with a ghostly figure standing behind her, representing the assassinated President Lincoln.) Most people believed that the camera could not lie, and so could not be used to mislead people – a difficult

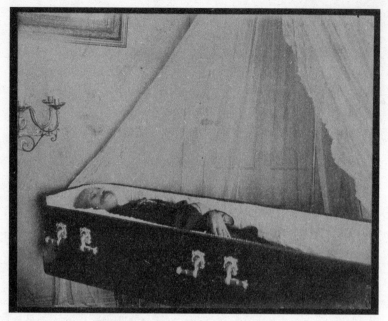

The front image for the 'corpse directions'.

view to relate to in this age of CGI technology. Spirit photography quickly became popular and gained supporters, including Arthur Conan Doyle, who wrote a defence of it. People would sit for portraits, and when the portrait was developed, their departed loved one would magically appear behind them – or with them – a corpse-less memento mori. This new sort of mourning ephemera made it seem as though the dead were watching the living, rather than the other way around, as Jen Cadwallader puts it. Time and space collapse, and the living participate for a moment with the dead – who seem to be still living, still aware, still watching.

If you find it hard to believe that so many people could have been taken in by these photographic hoaxes, don't forget that two processes were happening simultaneously. Firstly, the

Victorians were looking for a way to reframe death in a society where religion was rapidly losing ground. Secondly, the people who most sought out these spirit photographers were grieving and looking for answers. Spiritualism still had status as a pseudo-science, and in this culture of remembrance – where death and grief were public or glorified – portraits taken with the dead, or with their supposed ghosts, did not seem morbid. Ghosts are always with us, in memory if not in fact, and for the Victorians the line between life and death, science and spirit, was indistinct. Memento mori photographs could preserve the image of life and could even create the illusion that the subject was alive *when the photo was taken*. In the famous poem by William Wordsworth, a small child insists that 'we are seven', meaning she and all her brothers and sisters – counting the living and dead together.

'You say that two at Conway dwell,
And two are gone to sea,
Yet ye are seven! – I pray you tell,
Sweet Maid, how this may be.'
Then did the little Maid reply,
'Seven boys and girls are we;
Two of us in the church-yard lie,
Beneath the church-yard tree.' [. . .]
'But they are dead; those two are dead!
Their spirits are in heaven!'
'Twas throwing words away; for still
The little Maid would have her will,
And said, 'Nay, we are seven!'

A family photograph of both the living and the dead.

For the Victorian mourner, we are – even in grief – among friends and loved ones. We are never alone.

The death of death culture

Despite the popularity of Victorian death culture, the veneration of secular relics and the interaction with the dead through photography did not last. The industrial revolution was winding into high gear, and even the means of travel had begun to speed up. The steam engine became a symbol of both the good and bad aspects of progress. On one hand, steam was a brilliant invention that helped to modernise and connect Britain to her European neighbours; on the other, it ushered in an era of industrial catastrophe. Between the trauma of train crashes and the start of the Great War (World War I), the culture of grief shifted again. People stopped keeping locks of hair; they stopped recording slow death in their diaries; they stopped lingering over the dead or the deathbed. People rarely kept bodies in their homes – funeral parlours took on that job – and relics, so important for so long, lost both their meaning and their status.

Why this waning interest in memento mori happened is open to speculation. The Victorian grief culture may have fallen victim to the speeding up of life and the stripping away of the last vestiges of magic (including the séance, the para-psychology experiments, telepathy, belief in fairies). Sigmund Freud's theories would replace the sciences of mind that made room for object-memory, and by the end of the nine-teenth century, much of the relic culture of death had gone. What replaced it has changed both the way we live and the way we die today – it has changed how we see our own mor-tality, and how we approach the deathbeds of those around us (when – or rather if – we do). In the next chapters I will examine how the twentieth century, radically different from almost every age and culture that preceded it, devalued ritual at the same rate as religion, abandoning both for a greater emphasis on science and technology, disease categories, diag-nostics and labels. The screen of the hospital, which provides us with clinical distance from death and dying but also from one another, cannot offer us the communal storytelling that ritual provides. The modern westerner has lost *loss*; death as a community event, and mourning as a communal practice, has been steadily killed off.

And this, incidentally, is our inheritance.

Chapter 5

DEATH AT
THE ANATOMY
THEATRE

Anatomy, specimens and medical cadavers in the West

In 2013, the Case Western Reserve University School of Medicine and the Cleveland Clinic Lerner College of Medicine, both located in Cleveland, Ohio, announced plans to build a joint medical education building. The historic partnership will result in a state-of-the-art facility to the tune of more than eighty million US dollars. The plan is to be at the forefront of technology, a forward-thinking institution of the medical future. There is one thing that this new building will *not* have, however. There will be no cadaver lab for the purpose of human dissection.

This may be a recent development, but the decision by CWRU and CCLCM wasn't made in a vacuum. A brief search of medical journals – and indeed of the internet – reveals a sizzling debate. To quote the title of a 2004 debate forum in *The Anatomical Record*, 'To What Extent is Cadaver Dissection Necessary to Learn Medical Gross Anatomy?' That is, do we need a dead body to prepare medical students for practice? The forum was collegial, but not all discussions and rebuttals have been so friendly. Among medical faculty, the argument is not merely philosophical – and sometimes it simmers with bitter rancour. Human dissection has not, however, always been an element of medical training. In fact, the practice has been fraught almost since the first: a battleground over bodies, from the religious prohibition of the pre-modern period to a 'gory' New York City riot in the eighteenth century, when an enraged public rose up against bodysnatching anatomists. What do these tensions mean? How does the cadaver relate to conceptions of death, then and now? These questions have to do with more than medicine; they get at the heart of how we deal with death as an event (with a body) and dying as a process (with an overseeing physician) today.

Body of evidence

In 1832, five years before Queen Victoria took the throne, Britain passed the Anatomy Act. Its purpose was to increase the supply of cadavers for dissection. Bodies were needed, but the idea of dedicating one's body to science was still radical. 'Resurrection men', or men who purloined bodies from graves, had been hard at work for decades, and in 1828, two men by the name of Burke and Hare had literally 'made a killing'. The news broke on 3 November 1832; the 'most atrocious murders of the decade – of the century – had been committed' in Edinburgh's Old Town. William Burke and William Hare, together with Helen M'Dougal and Margaret Hare, killed sixteen people and sold their bodies to Dr Robert Knox, an anatomist. The investigation and trial, which is vividly brought to life by Lisa Rosner's *World of Burke and Hare* website, raised 'troubling questions' about how doctors got their cadavers. It did not, however, change the anatomists' conviction that cadaver dissection was necessary.

The Enlightenment belief in empiricism had helped to change seventeenth-century 'barber-surgery' into a science based on evidence. Students used to witness a master anatomist performing a dissection in an open theatre – this had, in fact, been the practice nearly from the first century on, instruction by 'watching' rather than 'doing'. By the eighteenth and nineteenth centuries, however, the medical student was expected to dissect a corpse, and that meant far more bodies were needed to meet the requirements of an expanding medical system. And so, the relationship between death and the doctor changed again. Rather than merely offering succour in the hour of death (the doctor's position up to the seventeenth century, for instance), or attempting to halt death's approach (the frequently hubristic attempts of the eighteenth century), the anatomist, as provider of empirical evidence in the form of a *body*, sees death as an opportunity.

It is difficult, now, for us to imagine the world of medicine before dissection. We must travel back a long way to see the entire picture: back to the first century AD. The work of Galen, a Greek physician and philosopher, came to prominence then as the primary source for anatomical instruction – even though he never dissected humans. How could this be? Galen performed vivisections of monkeys, dogs and pigs, and, with some educated guessing, used these mammal cadavers to develop a theory of human anatomy that was necessarily quite flawed. Regardless, his work became the primary text for use among medical students, and remained so *for 1,300 years*.

Picture the scene: a learned professor (who had probably never performed a dissection) would stand at a raised chair like a pulpit. From there, he would comment on the work of Galen, turning the pages and describing the organs while his assistants took apart a cadaver in front of a theatre of students, most of whom would never touch the body at all. In a popular BBC documentary series, Michael Mosley talks about the 'errors' of Galen – not really errors so much as misunderstandings based upon available knowledge – and notes that the presiding professors failed to comment on certain discrepancies even when they saw them – for instance, Galen claimed the human liver had three lobes, when it has only two. In the 1530s, however, change appeared on the horizon, thanks to the work of Andreas Vesalius, the 'father' of anatomy.

Vesalius ushered in a new approach to the practice and teaching of anatomy – but he, too, obtained his corpses by less than legal means. Often the bodies were of convicted criminals:

Andreas Vesalius (1514–1564).

on at least one occasion, the specimen was still hanging from the gibbet, and Vesalius pried loose the two rotting legs as they dangled above him. In Venice, Vesalius met artist Jan Stephan van Calcar, and by 1538 the two men had collaborated in the production of six 'fugitive sheets', or anatomical diagrams. In 1543, Vesalius published *De humani corporis fabrica libri septem* (*On the Fabric of the Human Body in Seven Books*), and – as stated gushingly by E. Ashworth Underwood – 'in an age when the dead hand of medievalism lay heavy on knowledge of the human frame, the whole science was born anew and advanced beyond recognition by the faith, the enthusiasm, and the unremitting labour of a single man.' We celebrated the 500-year anniversary of Vesalius's birth in 2014, and around the world his achievements are still being revisited. As a New York Public Library exhibit put it in 2000, covering seven hundred years of medical and scientific illustration, 'Seeing is Believing'.

Sophia Vackimes, a reviewer for the exhibit mentioned above, asks an interesting question: 'What were Andreas Vesalius or Hieronymus Brunschwig, author of *Buch der chirurgia* (c.1450–c.1512), thinking about while they presented the body as an object of scrutiny? Did they imagine that eventually it would be considered not as a whole entity but as numerous, cut-up bits and pieces?' It is a relevant question. After all, *how* we see and *what* we choose to display shape the world of medicine and science (and the body and death) as much as cultural beliefs construct the rituals performed within a given culture. And so, we return to the idea of the dead body as evidence: what kind of evidence is it? Does it matter that in the centuries after Vesalius bodies would not be drawn whole, but

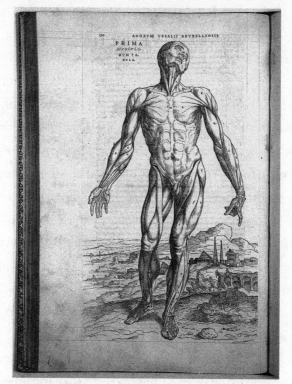

Diagram by Vesalius showing the major muscles in the body.

piecemeal? Does it matter that William Hunter would display a womb with child in his 1774 *Anatomy of the Human Gravid Uterus*, complete with bloodied cross-sections of the woman's legs, like two ham hocks? And does it matter that most of the bodies for dissection in the eighteenth century – in both the UK and the US – belonged to vulnerable populations? At the same time that the Victorians were carefully preserving bodies of loved ones in film and coiling their hair in jewellery, a trade in bodies began, in which the dead became coin of the medical realm – and bodysnatching a lucrative career.

Bodysnatching, you say?

In Chapter Four, I referred to the soft boundary between 'body' and 'thing'. The secularisation of death did not mean that the body no longer mattered, but that the sanctity and prohibition surrounding bodies began to lift. Death had been commodified by a grief industry principally interested in preserving and providing material goods, and so perhaps it is not surprising that the body itself became a sought-after commodity for medical study. What was the 'object' of that study, however? Increasingly, the chance to examine a dead body was considered to be the only means of gaining a necessary and proper medical education, especially for surgeons. Inevitably, more bodies had to come from somewhere, and the vulnerable lower classes were the easiest target.

The 1832 Anatomy Act intended to provide greater access to cadavers for medical science, but, as Ruth Richardson explains in *Death, Dissection and the Destitute*, it was viewed with fear and revulsion. Called the 'Dead Body Bill', the 'Dissecting Bill' and the 'Blood-stained Anatomy Act', it allowed the unclaimed bodies of paupers to be given to the anatomy schools. The 1834 Poor Law that followed added to the unease for the labouring poor in Britain. An article for the *Spectator* published in 1838 claims: 'If they were poor they imprisoned them, then starved them to death, and after they were dead they butchered them.'

Similar incendiary attacks were made in the US, both before and after the New York 'Doctors' Riot' of 1788. As many as twenty people died during the riot itself, which was sparked by a series of newspaper stories. In a Smithsonian article, 'The

Gory New York City Riot that Shaped American Medicine',
author Bess Lovejoy (*Rest in Pieces: The Curious Fates of Famous
Corpses*) remarks that a rash of media tales about grave-robbing
medical students helped to stir unrest. Most of these robberies
took place at Potter's Field and the city's so-called 'Negroes'
Burial Ground'. Lovejoy quotes from a petition in February of
that year: 'young gentlemen in this city who call themselves
students of the physic [. . .] under cover of the night, in the
most wanton sallies of excess . . . dig up bodies of deceased
friends and relatives of your petitioners, carrying them away
without respect for age or sex.' The practice of robbing graves
among poor and minority groups persisted, despite objec-
tions, well into the nineteenth century; John Harley Warner,
co-author of *Dissection: Photographs of a Rite of Passage in American
Medicine*, notes that in Boston in the 1840s, the influx of 'Irish
paupers' shifted the balance, though even in the twentieth century, African-Americans remained the primary 'at-risk population'. The New York riot – and the passage of subsequent
laws in the US – were driven, then, primarily by breaches in
this 'acceptable' practice of dissecting along racial and class
boundaries. As Lovejoy remarks, sentiments 'boiled over' in
New York when the body of a white woman was stolen from
Trinity Churchyard. Warner cites a similar example of public
outcry when the body of a former senator and son of President
William Henry Harrison was discovered (by his son, no less)
hanging in a dissection lab in Ohio in 1878. However, while
the bodysnatchers largely followed what a nineteenth-century
anatomist called the 'prudent line of stealing only the bodies of
the poor', the practice effectively continued unabated.

Securing the specimen

Anatomical specimens had become so necessary that Michael Sappol, author of *A Traffic of Dead Bodies*, claims the modernisation of medicine depended upon them. They must be procured *somehow*. Occasionally, students themselves might work to get a body, but in places where body trafficking was heavy, professional 'resurrectionists' held sway. The means of securing specimens may seem barbaric now, but could be very workmanlike; a good resurrectionist would have an extensive network that included undertakers, graveyard workers and even other doctors who might be called to the deathbed of a patient and so provide first notification. Warner gives details from the notes of a prolific Nashville resurrectionist: the process required three men and a wagon, and took about an hour in good weather; the coffin would be uncovered and the top broken to allow access to the body, which would be drawn forth by a rope tied around the neck. The bodies were stripped of incriminating identification and the dirt, flowers and other grave arrangements were replaced to disguise interference. In good times, says Warner, the resurrectionist would take 'standing orders', and in the US, an active interstate trade commenced – furnished almost completely by 'black bodies disinterred from southern graves'. In Britain, the practice was largely the same, though the at-risk population was the white poor. The graves of paupers were not deep and a single one might have as many as four bodies stacked on one another. Resurrectionists in urban areas worked late at night, using wooden shovels to avoid the tell-tale 'clank' of digging.

In much of the US, laws against grave-robbing were slow in coming (in Nashville, it wasn't officially outlawed until the twentieth century), and in Britain, the practice was a misdemeanour; only when an object was stolen from the body did it become a felony. But this raises an interesting question: clearly the body was treated as a commodity, and so seemingly objectified. But is the body itself an object? In other words, what, if any, sanctity remained for remains once in the hands of the anatomists? Buyers and sellers squabbled over the 'specimens', which were subject to supply and demand, and cadavers travelled about like the other goods produced by the industrial age. And yet, these practices, particularly in the US and in Britain, but also in France and other parts of Europe, took place concurrently with the culture of grief described in Chapter Four. The examination of the corpse may have brought about the modernisation of medicine, but it did not change the view of the horror-stricken bereaved. What we see instead is a contest of sorts between the medical professional and the public over the sanctity of death, and a real fear that dissection 'dehumanised' the doctor as well as the deceased.

The body and the human

Warner quotes a professor in Memphis as announcing that 'You are now upon that stage of life, when the formation of character is inevitable [. . .] your destinies be moulded, for good or evil.' The professors and the students themselves saw the risk of 'hardening', of developing a crust that inured them to human life and death, and this was considered particularly dangerous for women students. Victorian ideals suggested that women had unique qualities that suited them primarily for motherhood and wifehood. If they were to enter medicine, it ought to be as dutiful nurses and healers (though only until marriage; women were not permitted to pursue their careers once they tied the knot). Women were thought to be weaker physically but also morally – a continuation of the sentiments from the male-centric Enlightenment, which maintained that women could not and should not be educated, for fear of turning their brains and encouraging loose morals. Early pedagogues like François Fénelon, who influenced Locke, suggested that women were too 'Fickle' and had a 'Softness and Timorousness', which rendered them 'incapable of firm and regular Conduct'. (It's little wonder that Locke's own treatises about human freedom contained a conspicuous blind spot as they pertained to women.) Despite improvements to women's station, anatomy professor John Ware declared in 1860 that dissection defiled a woman's 'moral constitution'. This challenge was answered, however, by Emeline Cleveland, professor at the Woman's Medical College of Pennsylvania, who declared the study of anatomy a 'hymn in honor of the creator'. So what did this mean for the anatomists, male and female, as they approached their education in life and death? If the study of anatomy threatened to harden women, with their supposedly softer sentiments, what did it do to men? Would it harden the attitude of any anatomist to death, destroying likewise the sanctity of life? Despite Dr Cleveland's statement to the contrary, that remained a real fear.

A different kind of memento mori

Both John Harley Warner and James Edmonson (curator of the Dittrick Museum) comment on the humanity – or not – of the dissection room in *Dissection: Photographs of a Rite of Passage in American Medicine 1880–1930*. This remarkable volume contains some of the Dittrick's extensive collection of dissection room photographs. In today's cadaver labs, photography is strictly prohibited, and phones are confiscated before entry to remove temptation. But in the nineteenth century – and particularly in the US – a virtual craze for dissection-room photos swept anatomy labs. Prior to the 1800s, Europe had 'superior access' to corpses, and students travelled to London, Paris and Vienna. By the 1850s, in-person dissection was not only the norm, it was a pivotal moment, a rite of passage – a thing worth memorialising. Unlike memento mori photographs of the dead, these images made the division between living and dead apparent, even morbidly so. They were, however, just as artfully arranged.

One of the Dittrick's images is a photo of famed Cleveland surgeon Gustav Weber. The image, on a cabinet card, has been arranged to look almost like the paintings and iconography of the fifteenth century. In fact, Weber owned a romanticised portrait of Andreas Vesalius, and Edmonson suggests that this iconography may have served as a kind of inspiration. Another famous painting that bears a familiar relationship to the dissection photo is Rembrandt's *The Anatomy Lesson of Dr Nicolaes Tulp*. Both examples imply that a precedent existed, but now there was a sudden and remarkable immediacy – and

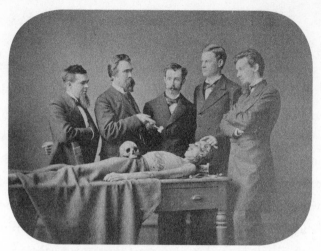

Group photo of students in a dissection room.

by 1900, the development of Kodak's 'Brownie' camera allowed photos to be reproduced as postcards. But the question remains: why? Why would students wish to memorialise gross anatomy – particularly since the practice was still seen as horrific by the public, and the memory of riots and revolts was still fresh?

Despite encouraging students to remember that the body they dissected was once a living being, and despite Emeline Cleveland's suggestion that the practice might make one more, rather than less, aware of the divinity of creation, many of these photos of dissected corpses border on disrespectful, even violent. The body's parts lie open; sometimes a disembodied hand holds a cigarette. Grinning students grip heads, make bodies stand with them, arrange them to play poker or put them on greeting cards to family members. The images occasionally bear inscriptions like 'a bunch of vultures working on a cadaver', or worse, racial slurs. They seem to play into the public's worst fears, as though students embraced the grim role assigned to them – and certainly the Burke and Hare trial in Britain did nothing to lift the stigma. On the other hand, these same photographs tell a second story. In this tale, the body becomes the subject rather than the object. Really, we are looking not at anatomy, but at *anatomists*.

In this image, we see the anatomy student once more in a crowd of witnesses. This time, however, it is he who remains under scrutiny, and the presiding figures watch over him with cold, unseeing eyes. The doctor is to be dissected, seemingly by death itself. These strange images (and there are a number of them in the Dittrick collection) may be part of the 'tomfoolery' of medical students, but they also offer a blurring of boundaries between life and death. To lie upon the table, knowing what the table represents, would have been a serious undertaking.

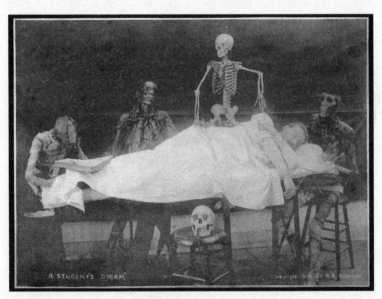

A prank photograph depicting a medical student attended by cadavers.

Some have names, like 'A Student's Dream', that represent an identification with the dead. To change places with a corpse is not the same as to pose with a corpse; even memento mori photographs that pose dead and living children together do not accomplish the same level of identification. This is a 'putting on' of death, a recognition that if the corpse is mere object, then *so am I*. And here we once more approach the delicate and scarily permeable boundary: am I separate from the dead? Do the dead linger near, do they still have an effect, still watch with accusation and – possibly – with otherworldly influence? The tether between the living and the dead that was partly severed by the Reformation's movement away from Catholic death rituals re-forms in new ways.

The memento mori of the medical theatre may not be the same kind of memorial as the parlour photograph, but it *is* a memorial. Gross anatomy became, for these students, a rite of passage. All encountered it equally. It was a shared experience of teamwork and team play, pitting the students against a wider world that could not understand their gruesome work. Anatomy may have played a role in revolutionising medicine in terms of practice, but it also unified a disparate field, giving them common ground (and sometimes common enemies). In *Dream Anatomy*, Sappol suggests that the ritual acquired a kind of mystique because of its 'wilful transgressions of funeral custom' – that, as the 'preeminent ritual that inducted young men into the fraternity of knowledge', dissection ultimately became a type of 'death cult'. From Vesalius's *Fabric of the Human Body* to William Hunter's *Gravid Uterus* to the photographs taken by anatomy students, seeing the inside of a body became central

to treating its ailments. The dead body teaches doctors a great
deal but the lesson, ironically, is *not* about death.

A body apart

If anatomy does not teach us about death, what place does
it have in our understanding of death today? The anatomists
of the nineteenth and early twentieth centuries cautioned that
the study of a piecemeal body actually desensitised the student
to death, and possibly stunted his ability to relate to his fellow man. The worry: modern medical practice may be making excellent doctors, but it was also turning out imperfect
humans. By the 1920s, dissection practices, though not wholly
public, had gained currency in the public consciousness. As
Warner reminds us, though, this very familiarity 'contributed
to a legacy of distrust', particularly among minorities. Anatomy
labs responded to the criticism by embracing a sense of detachment; students were to take the practice of dissection seriously
– no jokes, no more 'tomfoolery', but also none of the emotional resonance that Dr Cleveland had lauded as its hallmark.
Reforms intent on 'humanising' the profession gave rise to
what Warner describes as 'a new convention of silence', where
feelings, particularly those of the doctor-in-training, were to
be denied. The cadaver lab, one of the only places where the
dead body exists for the sole purpose of instruction, actually
removes some of the boundary-blurring reflection that had,
at least partly, informed the dissection photograph (and the
photographs themselves became a thing of the past). What, in

this encounter, was lost – and how it might be found – became the subject of additional reforms that spread across the US in the 1960s and 1970s, as people searched for a way to ensure that the dying did not lose their humanity at the hands of their doctors. After all, what *exactly* does a body in pieces teach us?

In Chapter One, I told the story of my first encounter with the event of death. The man had been living moments before, eating, reading the paper. He was a person. As we worked to revive him, he did not – for me – cease to be a person. When I knew we had failed, the man made a sort of transition in my brain from live person to dead person, but his humanity was never in question. When I returned to the diner to ask about the outcome of the incident, I asked about the *man* not the body. And none of this should be surprising.

However, imagine, instead, an organ preserved in glass. The Mütter Museum of Philadelphia has many such objects, as do the Royal College of Surgeons' Hunterian Museum and Bart's Pathology Museum in London. The Berlin Medical History Museum also has pathological and anatomy specimens, and another significant collection resides at Leiden University. Some of these are teaching collections, others mainly histori-cal. But what do we learn from visiting and viewing? Does a pancreas in a jar offer the same experience as seeing a dead body? If you enlarge the scope and imagine instead a nerv-ous system on display, or a vascular system (I have seen both), you get a sense of the whole body, but still the tangle of vein or nerve is unlikely to register as a human being. Skeletons, then – what of them? We have one at the Dittrick Medical History Center, in a 'closet', no less (he hangs in a cabinet in the 1875 Doctor's Office Period Room). Here is the scaffold upon which all of us are built, but I find few visitors have more than a passing reaction to the articulated bones. Perhaps it's due to the ubiquity of skeletons in art (and in certain holiday celebrations); perhaps it has to do with the denatured quality of dry bones. When I take my classes to the bone lab at the Cleveland Museum of Natural History – the valuable Ham and Todd collection – there is some amount of awe related to the sheer magnitude, but still, no sense of the 'person'. Somehow, a body 'a-part' is also a body 'apart'. We do not relate to it the way we might to a whole body, still seemingly intact, but no longer 'with us'. The approach to death makes no inroads to our consciousness without the additional sense that memento mori implies: 'remember you, too, will die'.

Dr Sappol notes the attempts of early anatomy texts to 'shock' the reader, and even the pleasure of that shock; the sense that there was an erotic power wielded by anatomists and anatomy artists in 'undressing' the body. This was not universally true, of course; Jan van Rymsdyk, who illustrated the eighteenth-century atlases for William Smellie and William Hunter, suffered something akin to a breakdown from the hours spent hovering over dead women and their children with his palette of chalks. Regardless, the shock remains primarily for the outsider, unprepared for a look into the body – and a similarly interesting tale has been told about the first X-rays. In 1895, when Wilhelm Conrad Röntgen X-rayed his wife's hand, the darkened glass did more than reveal the bones beneath her flesh; the connection between 'person', 'self' and the denatured 'skeleton' suddenly collided. The technology spread rapidly, appearing around the world in a manner of months. Never mind that seeing the inside of your own body can be highly unsettling; the eagerness to 'see' drove innovation, and in Cleveland, Ohio, Dayton C. Miller made the first composite (that is, whole skeletal image) in the same year that Röntgen released his findings.

Although the funeral industry tends to keep us at a distance from the body and its grave preparations, it is interesting that in other contexts, when there is an opportunity to 'see the body', most of us want to look. The often-debated *Body Worlds* exhibition of Gunther von Hagens stands as proof that we will in fact *pay* to look. But in that exhibition, the parts have been reassembled in everyday action, returning us (visually speaking) to the works of Renaissance anatomists who show cadavers standing, dancing, pointing, playing. Some have accused von Hagens of grotesquery, sensationalism and worse, comparing his works to the 'freak shows' that were so popular, interestingly, in the Victorian era. Others consider his work a unique contribution to our own understanding of mortality and the body, a taboo-breaking event of epic, if market-driven, proportions. I will come back to von Hagens later, but regardless, the effort to bring the 'human' back to the dissected 'body' has also been prevalent in dissection labs for the past few decades. 'Detachment', Warner remarks, citing critics from the late 1970s, might actually 'work *against* professionalism', might translate to equally inhumane treatment towards the patient in illness – and in death.

Elisabeth Kübler-Ross wrote *On Death and Dying* in 1969, partly to expose and partly to provoke improvement of the poor training doctors received in dealing with dying patients and their families. The book rapidly became a bestseller. In the *British Medical Journal*'s tribute to Kübler-Ross, the book's transformative model of grief was described as literally 'rocking' the medical profession and resulting in a public outcry for 'compassionate care' for the dying. Kübler-Ross noted that, in Switzerland, death and birth were considered part of the life cycle and not something to be overseen by medicine or technology. In that sense, the Swiss model was similar to other cultural and historical understandings of the 'naturalness' of death and dying. Most people in Switzerland died at home surrounded by family, rather than at the hospital surrounded by machines and doctors. Kübler-Ross refocused, once again, on the concept of the 'good death', so popular centuries earlier. The idea of comfort and calm at the end had been lost over the decades, its disappearance partly attributed, she felt, to medicine and the medical treatment of the body before and after death. Her famous five-stage framework (denial, anger, bargaining, depression and acceptance) still has resonance, even though – as nearly all 'frameworks' for dealing with personal experience – it proved far too simple. Regardless, *On Death and Dying* reunited, in some ways, the divergent paths of anatomy students and the wider culture within which they existed. Doctors, who had the 'special' hard-won knowledge of dissection drawn from Vesalius, the grave-robbers and the cadaver labs of the nineteenth and early twentieth centuries, once again confronted a public outcry for greater humanity. How and in what way should emotion be reintroduced to the delicate boundary between life and death, patient and cadaver?

Through the use of idealised, piecemeal, intensely coloured images, says Sappol, anatomy lost its association with death. He says something else, however – that we have likewise lost our association with *mortality*. We buy aspirin, he explains, to protect us from the experience of physical pain, and similarly, we pay for 'health and funerary professionals to place a veil between us and death, and the dead body'. Even the *Body Worlds* exhibit, which is entirely composed of dead bodies, denies death. In fact, possibly the most compelling aspect of von Hagens' displays is their lifelike presentation. The figures run, they play soccer, they dance. He is able to produce them through 'plastination', a process he patented, which replaces the fluids and fats with a reactive polymer that makes them odourless and durable. The bodies are selectively dissected, then posed, then gas-cured, resulting in vibrant colour and a hardness that allows them to stand on their own (something no other sort of corpse can do). In *Dissection on Display*, Christine Quigley remarks that it's partly these 'posthumous personalities' that draws crowds; von Hagens does not 'intend plastinates to be viewed objectively', and encourages an emotional response. Even so, this is not necessarily a response to death. The figures seem to be living, carrying on in their after-death as they did before, and neither haunting us (as with the Black Death's *danse macabre*) nor cajoling us, or serving as a reminder of our common end.

In some ways, the new anatomies provided by books or by digital demonstrations of the body are as stoic and detached as the anatomist was once expected to be. Medicalised anatomies don't directly engage us, Sappol suggests, in part because to play with the dead would be considered the height of disrespect. The *Body Worlds* anatomies may engage us, but are not part of the medical theatre. The cadaver is travelling again, not *to* medical schools but *away* from them – and that returns us to where we began: what of the corpse-free anatomy lab?

Disembodied medicine

Experts at Australia's Melbourne and Monash Universities recently unveiled 'Anatomedia'. This software claims to be a 'comprehensive, self-paced learning programme that explores anatomy from four different perspectives'. It simulates dissections and post-mortems, providing detailed scans of real bodies and labels to describe the sections, organs and more. For a more hands-on approach, the company SynDaver™ Labs constructs simulated tissue, organs or whole bodies for dissection. Their 'Synthetic Human' includes skin with fat and fascia, bones, muscles, tendons, ligaments, articulating joints, a functioning respiratory system, a complete digestive system, visceral and reproductive organs, and a circulatory system. The goal of SynDaver™ is to replace human cadavers in medical education and training with 'synthetic analogs' that are, as their mission statement explains, 'more cost-effective than the relevant animal or human model'. In addition to replacing the 'dead' body, SynDaver™ hopes to develop synthetic humans that breathe, bleed and react to stimulus, with both synthetic and 'living' cells. These are just two types of 'bodiless' anatomies – and just the most recent. Earlier equivalents did exist,

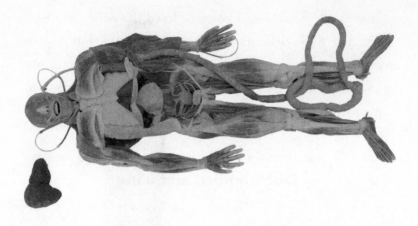

'Synthetic Human' by SynDaver™ Labs.

from so-called 'wax Venus' obstetric models to more robust papier-mâché models, and each attempted to do the same thing: replace the body.

The 'Josephinum Museum' of the Medical University of Vienna, Austria, houses the second-largest collection of wax anatomical models in the world, and the largest collection of wax obstetric models. In a world where cadavers were difficult to come by and decomposed swiftly, the wax anatomies of the seventeenth and eighteenth centuries offered replacements that multiple students could use for training purposes. Unfortunately, such objects could not truly be handled; the soft wax would deform under the pressure and heat of many fingers. Excellent for viewing, the wax models compared (in a sense) to the digital anatomies of today. More hands-on body replacement came in the form of papier-mâché models.

Dr Louis Thomas Jérôme Auzoux (1797–1880) began manufacturing anatomical figures in the late 1820s. These

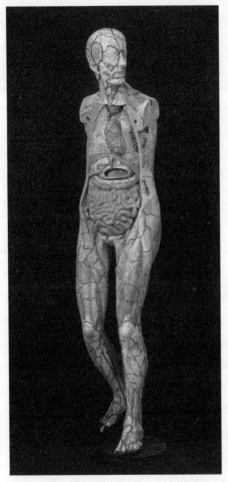

Anatomical figure for 'dissection'.

models incorporated virtually every anatomical feature and could be 'dissected' methodically. The individually numbered parts, all painted to resemble actual human anatomy, were keyed to an accompanying chart so students could positively identify and name each structure, muscle, bone and organ. A full-size male figure constructed around 1830 included over 125 separate parts, with 1,100 numbered anatomical details.

Auzoux later branched out to make models of individual anatomical structures (for example, the eye or the female reproductive system), veterinary figures and biological and botanical models, with a mission not very different from that of SynDaver™ Labs. Why, then, have current anatomical-replacement innovations sparked such angry debate? There are no easy answers; if anything, there are additional questions. A look at both sides demonstrates just how much ideas about anatomy have changed, but also how different our approach to bodies, and to death, has become in a medical age.

On Halloween 2013, the Dittrick Museum hosted medical historian Dr Lindsey Fitzharris. Her talk, 'Medicine's Dark Secrets', aimed to tell the human story behind medical specimens. Unravelling this sometimes sad and indisputably peculiar fate takes Fitzharris's investigation down a curious, unusual path – and she described her own first encounter with a medical cadaver. It was the hands, she remarks, with their painted fingernails, that drove home the idea that *this was a person*. Mary Roach, in her brilliant book *Stiff: The Curious Lives of Human Cadavers*, cites a similar story:

'One young woman's tribute describes unwrapping her cadaver's hands and being brought up short by the realisation that the nails were painted pink. "The pictures in the anatomy atlas did not show nail polish', she wrote. 'Did you choose the colour? Did you think that I would see it? I wanted to tell you about the inside of your hands. I want you to know you are always there when I see patients. When I palpate an abdomen, yours are the organs I imagine. When I listen to a heart, I recall holding your heart." '

For Fitzharris, for the anatomist quoted by Roach and for many others, this moment in the dissection room is pivotal for the same reason it was pivotal for the Victorians – as a rite of passage (and they describe it the same way). There are others arguing for continued cadaver dissection, however, who regard it as something more – even as the foundation of knowledge.

Dr Rosser, the head of anatomy and cell biology at the University of Saskatchewan's College of Medicine, says medical students will miss out on something 'fundamental' if they are not required to dissect: 'It's like the difference between watching somebody show you how to drive a car, and actually driving it.' Rosser also calls dissection the gold standard for teaching anatomy – and many feel the same. In a study by Horst-Werner Korf et al. titled 'The Dissection Course – Necessary and Indispensable for Teaching Anatomy to Medical Students', nine arguments are given for the continuation of cadaver lab dissection. 'When I cut at this site, I normally should see this or that,' the writers explain. 'If such is the case, then you have learned something. If something unexpected emerges, then you have also learned something.' Plastinates or anatomical models, the authors argue, 'do not allow such a way of thinking' – and, more troubling, 'the difference between "production" and "discovery" is denied.'

As part of an invited debate in the *Anatomical Record*, Dr Noelle A. Granger argues, further, that 'real' bodies change as they age. It is in the dissection laboratory, she explains, that students 'form their ideas and mental images of the structure of the human body at different levels over time'. Routine dissections also, Granger claims, familiarise students with tools and procedures, and cannot be replaced by synthetic means. Other claims put forth by proponents of dissection include some that we've already addressed: seeing is believing, practice makes perfect and the sense that dissection knowledge for the medical student ought to be standard (and not just for surgeons) – that it ought to be a rite of sorts.

Another argument, occasionally veiled in the debate but presented with some clarity in the Korf article, is the subject/object divide. Bodies are objects, Korf and his colleagues claim, while patients are subjects, and only dissection teaches students how to cross that boundary. The 'first arduous step required of students in dissection courses is the cold objectivism of the cadaver', they claim, and the dissection *reveals* the subjectivity forensically, telling the story of how that body lived and died. For Korf, as for Fitzharris and many others, the body *is* the story – even if only told to the anatomist.

Cadavers are still a kind of commodity, and still very pricey. Nowadays medical donation makes it unnecessary to buy the dead, but keeping the cadaver housed properly brings with it enormous expense. The ducts and air circulatory systems must be specially engineered, the space needs to be available to start with, and even when all of these items are in place, part of the medical curriculum must be dedicated to anatomical practice. Kimberly Todd, in response to Granger's article, remarks that cadaver dissection is *not* universally necessary to all students, and in fact might be misleading to some, because embalmed cadavers lose important features like joint cavities through deterioration. Todd argues, too, that all the same lessons (teamwork, language, familiarisation with tissues and tools) can be accomplished without full-body dissection. John Bertram, coordinator of anatomy teaching at the University of Calgary's faculty of medicine, points out that the curriculum is already heavy and new material must take the place of something else; in a programme where more than 50 per cent of the students go on to family practice (instead of surgery), cadaver dissection may be usefully 'cut'. Synthetic cadavers keep costs down, and since specialists like surgeons go on to do many dissections in their future training, those in favour of removing gross anatomy from medical schools suggest it is merely a holdover from a bygone era.

Nothing 'new' is discovered in anatomy; rather, it is a 'new' experience for students. Emmanuelle Godeau MD, PhD, of the French Institute of Health, suggests that, after all, dissection may have come to be *primarily* a rite of passage, and only incidentally instructive about anatomy. In an anthropological study, Godeau found that one hundred medical students and doctors from France, Italy, Switzerland and the US support the *idea* that dissection is necessary – but that it is an 'ambiguous necessity'. Citing dissection as a 'privilege' denied to non-doctors, Godeau concludes that 'behind the doors of the anatomy lab', dissection separates 'those who will become doctors from those who will not, those who have managed to control their senses from those who did not succeed, those who have overcome the horror of death from those who have not been confronted with it and never will be' – at least, he clarifies, *not as a doctor*.

What does it mean to confront death? In our collective history, acquaintance with the dead and dying as a rite of passage belonged to the living community who prepared the dead for their after-journey. The 'passage' referred to the boundary between worlds, a line all would cross eventually. Death specialists did exist, and still do; the Tibetan sky burial could not be completed without the undertaker whose job it is to 'dissect' at the funeral. One of the most important elements of a proper Jewish burial is the *Tahara*, a burial ritual of dignity performed by the Chevra Kadisha, or sacred burial society. There are many other instances of death mediated by those specially trained for it, from the priests of pre-Reformation Europe to the funeral directors, morticians and undertakers of today. And yet today we rarely hear of such practices described as rites of passage.

There are, I suggest, two reasons for this. First, for these specialists, death is a profession, not a fleeting part of medical education. Second, the services rendered here, even, I think, for the Tibetan undertaker, are part of the life–death cycle. There is no getting 'beyond' the body; it remains the site of death, as it was once the site of life – a reminder of our shared mortality. Death unifies a community in its humanity, while dissection unifies doctors as a separate group within that community. The anatomy lesson was deritualised, only to return again as a more symbolic kind of learning, a rite of passage many doctors do not wish to go without.

Regardless of which side of the debate you support, whether you understand gross anatomy as the best means of teaching medicine or as a relic reduced to symbolism, one thing remains clear: most of us are not doctors. Younger westerners who have not attended a dissection class are unlikely to have seen a corpse – a dead body uncovered, unadorned and unmediated – in any other context. The screen of distance from the dead, be it through the hospital room, the funeral parlour or the digital medium, changes our understanding of death. In a future of medical schools without cadaver labs, even medical students may be at one remove from the body. The synthetic corpse offers definite advantages as a teaching tool, with its clean, bright, clinical tissues. The posed plastinate hides the flabby inertia of decaying flesh. At this remove, though, who will understand the messy, frustrating, body-disrupting quality of death if even the medical profession is shielded from this reality? And – perhaps a more pressing question – who will be able to cope with the messy, frustrating, body-disrupting quality of *dying*, or of *grief*? The West lives in a medically mediated age, but even so, death comes.

How then, should we meet it?

Chapter 6

DEATH AND THE DOCTOR

Behind the screen of palliative care

'For God's sake, transfuse her!'
Panic rings in the man's voice; his wife has suffered major blood loss and fights for life as haemoglobin levels drop below 3 grams per decilitre. She has been rushed to ICU, dangerously close to death by exsanguination, but the doctors will not perform the transfusion. It's the stuff of nightmares: a family pleading, a husband watching as physicians stand by – but, despite appearances, the patient is not the victim of discrimination or malpractice. She has, in many ways, orchestrated this moment by signing an informed consent document prohibiting blood transfer, which violated her beliefs as a Jehovah's Witness.

The story above, told to me by my friend Michael DeGeorgia, a University Hospital neurologist, doesn't just describe a painful and frustrating scene in the ICU. It opens a window onto the complex relationships between physicians and patients, medical systems and mortality. Modern dying is managed dying, and it occurs in a culture of service provision and frequently competing expectations. In the Introduction, I asked some pressing questions: what has changed about death in Western culture? Has modern medicine 'sanitised' death? Or, possibly more problematic, has modern medicine given us the illusion of immortality? That is, have doctors stood in the way of our approach to death and our ability to accept it?

In some ways, that question is unfair – not because it isn't meaningful, but because it limits our perspective. The idea of medicine stepping in to control or otherwise mediate illness

Death and the Doctor (1744) by J. R. Imhoff Basel.

and death can only exist in a country with a large medical system and a class stratification that can afford to pay for it (especially in the US, where socialised medicine is slow in coming and frequently vilified). The dance of death and doctor has always been by invitation only; physicians appeared at deathbeds with increasing frequency by the seventeenth century, but only for the well-to-do. Today, in the West, that stratification still exists, but we can't deny that for many people the hospital will ultimately represent their final destination. Are doctors, therefore, the final mediators? If so, should they be? And if not – well, what then?

Natural death revisited

The doctor's role traditionally consisted of relieving pain and anguish as much as possible. Before the divergence of professions, a medical doctor might also be a counsellor, standing in for what today would be the psychologist as an extension of the 'pastoral' role, a fatherly figure who had your best interests at heart. In the Dittrick Museum collection we have the saddlebags of Dr Peter Allen, who covered miles of the Western Reserve of Connecticut (now northern Ohio) to visit his patients in the early 1800s. Still largely wilderness, the area around Cleveland bristled with small farms and home-steads; few could travel to the urban centre for treatment, so treatment came to them. The bags are tattered, blackened and well-worn. Inside them are vials and packets of medicine that Allen made himself and wrapped in newsprint. Allen knew his patients and their ailments intimately and, as doctor, coun-sellor and pharmacist, employed his collected knowledge to their benefit. Another doctor from the Western Reserve, Jared Potter Kirtland, planned to leave medicine after losing his wife and two children to typhus fever – but was so moved by the needs of his community that he continued to practise, travelling through treacherous terrain in order to treat another epidemic of the fever in the 1820s. These doctors are joined by hundreds more in the US and Europe – men (and notable women) who risked their lives to provide care and to improve the welfare of their patients. They fought outbreaks of cholera, smallpox, polio, diphtheria and typhus, not to mention the usual death by old age or accident and injury; and when all else failed, they paternally and professionally managed the dying. As we moved further away from the old understanding of death's inevitability, though, human beings began to fear it as an enemy – and the medical system joined the fight against death at our request, all 'natural death' movements aside.

Death *still* comes, but, as Dylan Thomas wrote, we 'do not go gently into that good night'. The curtain closes upon the fluttering pulse of life, and we deny it, fight it, find it unbearable. Regardless of whether a death was expected or even 'timely' due to age and infirmity, who in that moment of separation can truly say 'this is natural – it is as it should be'? In 1969, feminist philosopher Simone de Beauvoir wrote, 'there is no such thing as a natural death [. . .] All men must die: but for every man his death is an accident and, even if he knows it and consents to it, an unjustifiable violation.' To talk in the abstract about death, as I do here, remains at one remove from feeling it; for when we feel it, there may be no words sufficient. The ringing, ragged sadness of poetry and fiction and painting may be the closest we can come: 'No, no, no life!' cries Shakespeare's King Lear over the body of his daughter Cordelia:

> *Why should a dog, a horse, a rat, have life,*
> *And thou no breath at all? Thou'lt come no more,*
> *Never, never, never, never, never!*
>
> (King Lear: Act V, scene iii)

Los Angeles photographer Andrew George recently worked on a project entitled 'Right Before I Die', where he captured the sentiments and photographs of men and women in their last days. One woman said, 'You run to the end of the diving board and jump off, into the black void, and hope that you land in water.' Another remarked: 'I'm not afraid to die – I'm afraid of what I've got to do to get there.' And another: 'more doctors and not much improvement'. At the moment of our own death, only we will have the experience, and sharing it will remain difficult, if not impossible; but what about all the other times we encounter death? Remember that death, for much of the world and for much of human history, was not a singular, individual moment but a community event. And remember, grief and ritual exist for the living as much as for the dying, perhaps more. A dying person dies to their family, suffers before their loved ones, expires before sobbing friends. *Do something!* they urge – *you're the doctor!* Hospital waiting rooms ring with the refrain 'it isn't right – it isn't fair – it isn't time'. Social historians suggest that death has lost its 'naturalness', but the medical care system may be a straw man. We have begun to demand more autonomy in the doctor–patient relationship, and we have different expectations as a result. This is especially true in the US, but the case of British child Ashya King, whose parents risked imprisonment by removing their son from NHS care in order to seek alternative medical treatment abroad, suggests that individuals in the UK are also demanding a greater say in their own care – as does the increasingly popular political mantra of 'patient choice'. That means necessarily moving away from the 'doctor knows best' system.

I want to return for a moment to the story of the patient dying of blood loss. 'Informed consent' and 'informed refusal' refer to the process of communication between patients and doctors about procedures they plan to undergo. The woman in question needed routine surgery, with a minor risk of blood loss. During a consultation, the woman explained that she was a Jehovah's Witness and, as a result, would not consent to a blood transfusion because according to their doctrine, this would violate the Judaic injunction against ingesting blood. Her husband disagreed with her, but neither he nor the doctor pushed the issue until she arrived in ICU on Dr DeGeorgia's watch. 'The truth is,' Michael explained, 'she had started attending the services mainly for the social contact and never really understood or bought into the theology but still she signed the form stating that she did not want any blood products in the event of an emergency.' Unwilling to violate the agreement, the resident doctors refused to do the transfusion, though Michael called and took part in multiple meetings with the treatment team, bioethics and legal advisement to try and sort it out. In the end, the doctors pulled her though *without* transfusion – but the ambiguity and a nagging shadow of doubt remained. Michael put it this way: if the heart of the Hippocratic Oath is, 'I will prescribe regimens for the good of my patients according to my ability and my judgement', what is my response and my responsibility to the patient?

If the woman had died, it would have been in one sense a 'natural death'. She needed surgery, she lost blood. In earlier centuries (even in earlier decades), her death would not have been a failure of medicine. Even so, she need not die today. Transfusion exists. To transfuse her would violate her religious beliefs, but might also save her life. Does this represent the pressure to use technology simply because it avails itself? Alternatively, was this a case in which the doctor should step back, as the 'death-midwife', and allow nature to run its course? Ultimately, the doctors prescribed a regimen of crystalloid infusion rather than blood, and the patient lived – but the questions remain. The relationship between death and the doctor seems muddier today than it has ever been. We need look no further than the present debates about assisted dying or 'do not resuscitate' notices; some patients want control over their death, and over their doctors. And yet the ethical quandary remains. If the Hippocratic Oath requires a doctor to give assistance – 'I will apply, for the benefit of the sick, all measures which are required' – are they wrong to withhold it when life is at stake? Or are they right to allow their patients to decide? And who decides which measures are required and which are not?

The social critic Ivan Illich made a comprehensive critique of medicine and dying in 1976, suggesting that doctors and the policies, organisations and technologies they followed or implemented led to disaster. Medicine could not deal with the messy and disorderly process of death, and so 'quieted' patients with medicine, potentially robbing them of the 'good death', where they had some agency. That intervention once seemed pastoral; in a modern context, however, critics argue that doctors and systems have 'butted in'. Suddenly, the hand of authority, perceived by historical predecessors as belonging to the Church, reappears as the hand of the doctor. If it wasn't for doctors, this argument goes, we would be free to experience death our own way. They have too long been the hoarders of specialised knowledge; medical systems, like megalithic powers and principalities, dictate too much. In Illich's critique, we see the rallying cry for a new kind of Reformation, one where the patient takes back responsibility for care, even when life and death hang in the balance. I have heard the arguments even now, in forums and online chat rooms, as comments on Ask.com and even in a thread on the *Daily Mail* website – and I, too, have suggested that hospital care can make it difficult for patients to be able to approach death in their own way. In *Celebrations of Death*, Peter Metcalf and Richard Huntington suggest that shying away from mortality is an especially marked feature of American medical culture, where hospitals must maintain the fiction that everyone will get better. Consider the 'cancer warrior' narrative that has become so prevalent in recent years – the constant focus on positive thinking amounts not only to a fiction but to a myth. It's not quite as straightforward as this argument might suggest, though. The doctor, the technology, even the miracle drugs cannot offer immortality – but in the contest over who has ultimate control, the patient may already have won.

Death's midwife?

We can't deny that medicine takes centre stage in nearly all important aspects of our lives. Despite the natural birth movement in the US, and despite the NHS midwifery service in the UK, many still seek hospital physicians for birth care (including the Duchess of Cambridge, who received a bit of backlash for it in the press). In the US, particularly, parents expect to give birth in the hospital, surrounded by the latest technology. In their article 'Midwives Among the Machines',

Raymond G. DeVries and Rebeca Barroso tell the story of a spontaneous birth that took place at a large American hospital. The woman, who was Hmong, opted to deliver on the floor, and an attending midwife assisted because the baby came before the doctor arrived. After the birth, the infant was aspirated – that is, had his stomach pumped – for no reason whatsoever, causing the nurse midwife to speculate that, because so much shiny technology surrounded them, it must be used. As the world changes around the health-care professional, say DeVries and Barroso, the professions must recreate themselves and their roles. This has been the case since the professions arrived on the scene, particularly at the twin poles of life and death. What drives technological improvements, research and development, and pharmaceuticals but the constantly shifting margin between illness and health – and, increasingly, life and death?

Medicine, I've remarked, began as the enemy of sickness and evolved instead to fight off encroachments of death for the adult, regardless of age. When all else fails, medicine aims to deliver the body from the pain of death, if not from death itself, and finally even to take away the pain of grief through psychiatric medicine. But if we think these innovations arrived at the behest of doctors, we are mistaken. They evolved from the often-invisible partnership between the doctor and patient which, never uncomplicated, has grown increasingly muddled in the internet age.

We desire patient autonomy – and so we should. But existing side by side with it we find something else, something I referred to in the beginning of this chapter: a call for doctors to get *more*, not *less* involved. In a 2012 article for the *Washington Post*, Craig Bowron talks about our 'Unrealistic Views of Death'.

An elderly patient suffers a stroke; the news is bad – and it must be delivered. And so the dilemma begins: 'If I'm lucky,' Bowron says, 'the family will recognise that their loved one's life is nearing its end. But I'm not always lucky. The family may ask me to use my physician superpowers to push the patient's tired body further down the road, with little thought as to whether the additional suffering to get there will be worth it.' No doctor actually possesses these magical powers, of course, and yet many have come to view death 'as a medical failure rather than life's natural conclusion'.

This view seems, however, to be contradicted by Professor John Ashton, president of the UK Faculty of Public Health and a proponent of the patient's right to die. In this scenario, the patient is ready, and it is the medical establishment that makes unreasonable demands. Ashton calls for doctors to serve as 'midwives' to the dying, helping them through the painful process – a suggestion picked up by numerous palliative care workers. Bronnie Ware wrote for the *Guardian* in defence of the midwifery idea, citing her work with dying patients. 'One powerful memory,' she writes, 'is from a patient named Stella, who grew incredibly frustrated with her inability to die despite her emotional readiness. It took her another month of suffering, despair and anguish before her body finally allowed her the release she longed for.' She goes on to say that, if patients make a rational request, then they ought also to be 'assisted' in the dying process – thus ensuring a pain-free or pain-limited death.

The easy end to suffering called for by Ware is actually a relatively recent phenomenon in the West. In a more pastoral age, most people hoped to be spared a quick death, as it prevented them from preparing for the end financially, socially and spiritually. By the Victorian era, and largely as a result of waning religious influence and rising gentrification, the old idea of the 'good death' had evolved to mean a quick and painless death. At the same time, a rise in medical intervention (and its successes) created a circular argument – if life can be preserved, surely it should be. Professor Ashton's position represents the most recent in a long history. In comments to the NHS, he put it this way: 'All over the country people are spending their last days and weeks in major discomfort because their medical carers are not willing to accept that it's the end of the line and to give them the necessary sedation to just speed things up a bit.' Death, like birth, will happen on its own – but a 'midwife' can make it far less painful and protracted. Why not, say Ashton and his supporters, do exactly that? Help them die, or at the very least, get out of their way and *let* them die. Anyone who has watched someone they love suffer can feel the tug of this argument.

And yet, it is never that simple. When is a patient making a rational choice? Who determines if they are in their 'right mind'? Who has the right to end a life? And frankly, when do we know – for a fact – that life is *over*?

Dead 'for all practical purposes'

It should be simple, shouldn't it? This person is 'alive'. That person is 'dead'. Among the Indonesian Torajans, of course, the line is fuzzier; someone is not officially dead until the funeral, and so despite the slow mummification of a corpse in the corner, Grandmother has not 'died' yet. The same might be said of the pre-Reformation Catholics, who believed a soul might return to help or hinder a relative – and can also be applied to the Victorian séances where the living sought to contact the dead in whatever nether region they inhabited. But surely *today* we have no trouble distinguishing the quick and the dead? As it happens, we do have trouble. Endless trouble.

Michael DeGeorgia, whose work in and out of the University Hospital emergency department often revolves around stroke and brain health, wrote an article called 'The History of Brain Death as Death' in 2013. In it, he dates this shift in living/dead diagnostics to 1947 and locates it specifically in Cleveland, Ohio, where cardiac surgeon Claude Beck famously 'defibrillated' the human heart, reversing certain death from cardiac arrest.

We are so used to this idea today – the resounding 'CLEAR!' and the shock of paddles, or CPR, which Beck developed – that it scarcely raises an eyebrow. But consider: at the time, Beck performed nothing short of a miracle. His achievement was followed in the 1950s by the invention and widespread use of ventilators, and taken in combination, these advances of technology meant a patient in a coma could be sustained artificially . . . and indefinitely. In short, a patient who would most certainly have died now 'lived', even if on life support. As Michael explains, however, this created serious ethical dilemmas. Did the patient suffer irreversible brain damage? Would they ever actually wake up? Were they not essentially dead already?

In the late 1970s, a car accident devastated the small Ohio town where my mother grew up. It tossed a young man through a windshield, dashed him against the asphalt, but did not kill him. My mother remembers the horror of it because she knew him; he was funny, full of life. He played practical jokes. He made you feel alive. And then, in his early twenties, he was struggling for life in the hospital. Life support kept him going, but he had lost all brain function. There is nothing so painful as the long wait, the endless hours of hopeful hovering, the sickening stretch of days and weeks and months when *nothing changes*. Years went by. One by one, friends stopped visiting. 'He was gone,' my mother explained. Gone and yet still there: 'We wanted to mourn, but we couldn't. It was so painful.' Unlike the situations described by Ashton and Ware, this patient was most assuredly not in 'his right mind'. He could not ask for this death; should it have been given to him anyway?

In 1954, Massachusetts neurologist Robert Schwab determined that heartbeat could not be counted on as the indicator of life. Instead, without reflexes, breathing or electroencephalograph (EEG) activity, a patient was 'considered' dead. In 1959, however, fellow neurologists Mollaret and Goulon disagreed, asking whether we could 'pretend to know the boundary between life and death'?

From the start, then, doctors struggled to agree on a definition of 'brain death'. We can plot the history from the 1950s to today, noting that even the original overseers of death and dying (in this case, Pope Pius XII in 1957) entered the debate. Pius decreed that physicians were not obligated to provide 'extraordinary' treatment in 'hopeless' cases; but how were doctors to determine hopelessness? In 1964, a colleague of Schwab's named Hamlin proposed death by EEG: no activity should mean no resuscitation. In 1968 an ad hoc committee gathered at Harvard to try and redefine death in a new way.

This 'new' definition did not offer much clarity, unfortunately: 'Any organ, brain or other, that no longer functions and has no possibility of functioning is for all practical purposes dead.' If anything, 'for all practical purposes' introduces an entirely different level of ambiguity – and the problems were compounded by differences between different nations. For instance, because of the UK emphasis on brain*stem* rather than EEG – which means a 'dead' (unresponsive) stem trumps any electrical activity that might show up – a patient could be considered alive in the US and dead in Britain. In 2007, the US President's Council on Bioethics discarded the word 'death' altogether, and replaced it with 'total brain failure', but even that is unhelpfully vague. Even more frustrating is that such terminology cannot account for the human element. In 2013, a thirteen-year-old American girl named Jahi suffered brain death after complications from a tonsillectomy. She was pronounced dead by the doctors, but her parents fought it with a court order. She remains on life support at a care facility in New Jersey, with her family and their lawyer fighting to have the diagnosis of 'brain death' recanted.

Jahi's family clusters around her; she is not 'practically dead' to them – nor was my mother's high school friend considered 'dead' by his mother, who moved him home and continued to care for him until his death by pneumonia. She insisted that her boy knew his friends when they came, though he never moved or responded. To her, he remained 'alive'. There are many stories like this, including a famous account from medical anthropology captured in the book *The Spirit Catches You and You Fall Down*. The story recounts a clash of cultures in which two Hmong parents (refugees from Laos) are charged with negligence in the care of their epileptic daughter, due primarily to errors of language transmission and a failure on the part of the medical community to recognise important cultural differences. The little girl, Lia Lee, ultimately suffered a grand mal seizure and slipped into a coma from which she never awoke. Her parents chose to take care of her themselves, chewing food and pressing it into her mouth. Having no brain function, Lia's body remained inert, transported around by her parents, who believed her soul had been taken on a journey to the spirit realm. Lia contracted pneumonia twenty-two years later, and only then, at the stopping of her heart, did her parents consider her dead. Here are three cases among many where the definition of death eludes us. Medical science cannot offer clear answers. Doctors can struggle to make correct care choices at the best of times, but when facing death, they find themselves nearly on equal footing with their patients.

In 2007 Pauline W. Chen published a revealing account of medicine's relationship with death, *Final Exam: A Surgeon's Reflections on Mortality*. In it, she chronicles her own deep anxieties about death and her inability to adequately relate to her patients about it. Though critics attack medicine as being too involved in the dying process, Chen tells a very different story. 'It never occurred to most of us,' she writes, 'that the actual process [of death] might be frightening, and that we could alleviate that fear by being present. And perhaps too, some of us – I include myself here – did not have the insight to realise that we were also leaving them alone because it was easier for us to stay away from the dying altogether.' This avoidance amounts, Chen believes, to a denial of death – but she isn't referring here to a belief in medical immortality. Instead, she refers to the very real fear all of us have of that common end. Another physician, Dr Elaine Goodman, recently wrote that the greatest medical lesson she had learned had nothing to do with training, and everything to do with her mother's death. My friend Michael has said much the same thing; you don't learn about death in medical school. The doctor learns about one form of death when he loses a patient, another when he or she is working on someone who dies – and yet another when his or her own parents begin to fail. In other words, doctors learn about death through experience, like everyone else. Death is the spectre that haunts and that shows up when you least expect it – and for Chen, that spectre even had a name. In Taiwanese, a restless soul is called *wan ong kuei*; after Chen 'turned away', as she tells it, from a patient she knew well as he succumbed to cancer, she felt haunted by him and by her choice.

If eighteenth-century physicians clung to the hubristic idea that they could end death, modern medicine seems much more likely to see death as an impending failure. And that tells us something very important. If the screen of palliative care makes it difficult for us to approach death, it's no easier for the doctors. Something behind the screen, behind and beyond the medical system itself, causes us to stumble in this most important task of the living: preparing for, understanding and greeting death, and helping others to die well.

Putting aside for a moment John Ashton's argument for doctor-assisted suicide, or the problematic life-support ethics of brain death, we need to ask: what are the expectations placed upon doctors by the patients they manage? A group called *Beyond Hospice* offers an 88-hour certificate training course for 'death midwives', but these are laypersons and not doctors. Why not? In America, a National Public Radio correspondent reported on how doctors 'learn to put death at arm's length', suggesting that medical training actually makes them less able to empathise with the grieving because they have to be able to leave death behind, 'at work' so to speak, and move on. We've heard that refrain before, from those in the early twentieth century who worried that dissection would harden the physician and make him less human. But in fact, future doctors may become more intimately familiar with the cadaver than they ever will with the thousands of patients they'll meet as residents. And that, says Michael DeGeorgia, is where 'you lose your sense of the human'.

Regaining the humanity of death: a doctor's perspective

The day was crisp for summer, a welcome break from the heat. Michael and I sat at a stone picnic table on the quad of Case Western Reserve University's campus. As a neurologist and lover of history, he has become my go-to for discussions of brain death, but I think it's also fair to call him one of life's philosophers. He is a thinker, and I consider him the soundest port in the storm of emergency medicine. I had asked him to meet for coffee weeks earlier, but in a quirk of scheduling fate, he'd been on call for weeks together and, here at his final day, looked beleaguered and exhausted.

'What would you like to know?' he asked.

To be honest, this turned out to be a harder question to answer than it sounds. I was about to ask a physician whether the medical system thwarted our attempts to approach death. I intended to ask, too, whether doctors had assumed the role of priest at the deathbed, in keeping with what social historians say about the modern shift from religion to medicine. But I began further back, with medical-school dissection labs and the lingering fear that doctors lost their sense of humanity and empathy through too-near association with corpses. He smiled, sipped his coffee and told me two stories. The first, about a Jehovah's Witness and the right to refuse blood transfusion, begins this chapter. The second concerned a man in his forties who suffered a torn artery and subsequent stroke while wrestling with his children. In both of these narratives, one thing stood out. The residents (junior doctors, or those in post-graduate medical training) seemed unconcerned about or indifferent to the patients involved.

'What I was frustrated with,' Michael recalled, 'is that nobody really seemed to care one way or another about this patient's decision to forego transfusion. To the residents, it was all cut and dried as long as she signed the form; they felt they were off the hook ethically and morally.' The young doctors did not feel an obligation towards the patient, and did not show concern over whether her decision was in fact a rational one – that is, made with a full understanding of the issue. That is not to say that personal or religious beliefs do not deserve respect; we should never try to see others through our own short-sighted lens, any more than we should judge each other's cultures or beliefs by our own limited experiences. The crux of the matter for Michael didn't concern the woman's religion, necessarily, but rather the apparent disinterest of her doctors in investigating or exploring the matter further. A similar situation occurred after the forty-three-year-old stroke victim Michael treated had been released. The prognosis seemed positive, but Michael wanted to check in on him. He stopped during rounds to call the man at home. Flummoxed, the residents asked why he would bother? Didn't he have better things to do? Michael's exasperated response: *this is someone's father, husband, brother*. Do not forget, he warned. Patients are not numbers, they are human beings.

What do these two stories reveal about modern medicine? It may be easy to malign the resident doctors, suggesting that nineteenth-century fears of doctors' lack of humanity had been justified. But Michael quickly defends them – and medical students, too. They put in thousands of hours and see thousands of patients; the fluorescent lights bleed colour from their faces as they walk the wards on little sleep and less nutrition. Depression hounds them. In 2013, an article in the *Wall Street Journal* suggested residents were 'dangerously exhausted', as the US limits for residents stands at eighty hours per week, including twenty-four-hour shifts. By comparison, Europe limits weekly hours to forty-eight, but as Rebecca Smith reports for the *Telegraph*, many medical students in the UK are being asked to 'opt out' and work more hours so that they gain enough experience to 'treat patients safely'. The number of hours required to learn – really learn – medicine shocks many people, and it requires the kind of fortitude we usually expect from people in military service. In fact, Michael compares medical students, and particularly post-graduate resident doctors, to soldiers suffering PTSD. 'You enter as a human,' he remarks, 'and years later, you get to be human again.' In between, the rush of new faces, each with similar conditions, creates a blur – it's little wonder residents think of their patients as numbers and not as names.

I've seen some of this first-hand. In 2013 and 2014, I helped to develop the Medical Humanities curriculum for the Cleveland Clinic Lerner College of Medicine. I've attempted to define this area of study in a number of ways over the years, but essentially, the medical humanities aim to reconnect medicine and the human. The Cleveland Clinic's course examines medical practice and medical systems from anthropological, historical, sociological and ethical perspectives. Think of it as a busy intersection: you have to pay attention to what you're doing, and it requires a lot of out-of-the-box thinking. I had bright students, but they struggled to complete the readings and other requirements, and during one seminar session, I asked them why. The answers varied, but essentially supported Michael's point. *I have no time for abstract thought – I can barely do what needs to be done as it is.* Today's doctors, especially in countries like the US, where the economy rests upon an ever-growing medical system, have been reduced to service providers.

What's wrong with medical service providers? In the US, doctors are even reviewed on websites like Yelp (a customer review site more commonly used to rate restaurants and so on). Isn't this as it should be? Doctors serve patients, after all. These are fair points; there may be nothing wrong with such a practice, so long as everyone understands the service model – as well as what has been gained and lost. Only fifty years ago, the doctor, like the father, knew best, and no one questioned him. As Kellehear describes it in his social history of death and dying, 'concerns over the struggles and agonies of the spirit soon gave way to the final struggles and agonies of the body and with the arrival of strokes, cancers and other diseases [. . .] the doctor soon replaced, or assumed equal power with, the priest as the darling of the deathbed.' There might not have been much choice, but people knew what to expect and who to turn to, and in turn, that fatherly role meant that doctors had responsibility, knew it and took it seriously. Today, roles have changed. Patients, with access to other patients across the globe and the odd, crowd-sourcing nature of WebMD, don't go to doctors for answers. They bring answers to the doctors, and expect options and service – in fact, they are encouraged to do so. The NHS encourages patients to research hospital rates, and insurance companies certainly want US patients to shop around. Do you want this treatment? Yes or no, depending on who will pay for it, perhaps. Michael's residents can't be faulted for merely ticking the box and concerning themselves with service provision (or not, as the case requires).

We seek absolute answers, but we don't always like what we hear; we do and do not want the doctor to have final authority. Doctors in their turn don't want to be 'wrong', especially in the US, where the cost of malpractice insurance is incredibly high as protection against lawsuits. Again, as we've thrown off the one-time authority of medicine in much the same way the Reformation rejected the ultimate authority of the priesthood, to what do we turn?

We have arrived at the heart of the matter. In this latest revolution, nobody wins. We haven't turned from one source of expert knowledge to another, but to the dispersion of knowledge through so many channels that it fans out and evaporates like a river in a floodplain. Those in the hospital waiting room *still want answers*, but increasingly there are no single recognisable authority figures to ask. You cannot fire the preacher and then ask him for a sermon. Perhaps this explains why so much of medical science revolves around life extension. We still look to find meaning in life and in death but, for many, the familiar rituals of our parents and grandparents simply no longer seem satisfying or meaningful.

The twin shifts of hospitalisation and state secularisation happened separately but concurrently. The irony? The more we disperse authority, listening to multiple and sometimes competing voices, the more we seem to lose our own. Locke's theories suggested that authority resided in the individual; throwing off the mantle of 'kings', be they political or religious, should increase each person's sense of individual power and authority. When it comes to death, however, we increasingly deliver the most important aspects into the hands of others.

These 'others' have, themselves, become diffuse, more like systems than individuals. Instead of the fatherly doctor who made medicines and travelled by horseback to treat patients, we find medical marts, alternative therapies, impersonal clinics, service providers and a quagmire of internet information. We've set sail into a sea of doubt without a compass, without a rudder – maybe even without *sails*. It's very difficult to arrive at your destination if you cannot even acknowledge where you are going. Small wonder most of us live in denial about mortality.

The long road home

The waiting room is wrapped in dreadful silence. Despite the attempt at cheerful decor, the bleach-white walls and low-ceiling light reflect everything in colourless dread. If the prognosis is bad, even the magazine covers seem to mock you. Somewhere, in a small room with tubes and technology, a loved one lies dying. You know it. No one tells you, you just *know*. To your right, a woman quiets her daughter with a toy. Further along, a man sits with his head in his hands. The doctor you saw yesterday isn't the one you saw last week – isn't the one you'll see today. Which of them will bring you the news? Will anyone tell you to go to the one you love, be with him or her at the end? Do you even want to? And what happens after that?

These questions frustrate and frighten us. Who, in that awful room, doesn't want a companion and comforter, someone who seems to have answers? We aren't wrong, necessarily, to expect that person to be the physician. At the same time, the doctor – frequently a product of the same culture – isn't going to be much better than a layperson. 'Medicine is facing a crisis,' says David Bornstein for the *New York Times*, 'but it's not just about money; it's about meaning.' Describing some of the same problems mentioned by Michael DeGeorgia, Bornstein claims that, while medical training 'formally' espouses the ethics of 'empathy, compassion and altruism', the underlying message for survival is 'stay detached, objective, even a little cynical'. This is certainly the attitude represented recently with television hits like *House* or *Bones*.

Dr Rachel Naomi Remen, clinical professor of family and community medicine and the director of the Institute for the Study of Health and Illness (ISHI) in Bolinas, California, describes her own early lesson in this 'hidden' curriculum: on her first day as an intern, a three-year-old died after an accident. When Remen cried as the parents were informed of the death, she was scolded by the chief resident as unprofessional. She learned the lesson so well that years later, she delivered the news of an infant's death to grieving parents with perfect composure and stoic distance. The father felt compelled to apologise for falling apart, and for the first time, Remen saw the consequence of that distance: she wasn't a comforter, but a strangely chastising burden to the grief-stricken. Remen went on to found the Healing Arts course at ISHI in an attempt to re-educate doctors with core values of compassion, service, reverence for life and harmlessness – and regardless of whether it makes doctors better at delivering bad news, the participants claim it helps keep them whole (and wholly human) throughout the desensitising process of medical training. DeGeorgia similarly recommends that residents spend time with hospice patients, volunteering their time to know, care for, ease and lose a person with whom they have a connection. But most of all, these programmes – and the obvious need for them – point to one thing: the doctor, just like the patient, just like the fearful family member in the waiting room, must learn to approach death.

In the West, in our modern age, we are helpless and lost in the wilderness of dying. Social historians note that, in some ways, we've arrived at the inverse of our ancestors' beliefs. No longer a 'place' and no longer a 'journey', the event of death represents a void, a nothingness or a kind of sweet release. By contrast, the *process* of dying frightens us with its dead ends, dangers, pain, suffering and confusion. The journey, says Allan Kellehear, is all on our side of life. 'Knowledge of the impending death may be uncertain,' he explains, and as a result, 'the journey is characterised by an unsettling, tiresome back-and-forth trajectory that is both wearing on all the participants and even, at times, shameful for everyone.' How could it be shameful? The type of death, of course, has something to do with it – the stigma, for instance, of HIV may still unfairly haunt the dying and their loved ones, while Alzheimer's robs the memory, the dignity and even the individuality of its sufferers before the end. But this shame comes in another way, as well. Life expectancy goes up, meaning diseases associated with old age happen to more people. Meanwhile, most people are treated in the hospital, and so the clinical setting mediates and blurs the decline of the body. But one day, the patient simply does not bounce back. And it's here that we find the shame-faced abandonment that can plague final hours, here where even the most faithful of friends and family might turn away, like Dr Chen with her patient, from the wreck of a body once beloved.

Even if you don't leave the bedside, even when you've done all that you can, guilt frequently remains. Grappling with death invites chaos and confusion, and this is made worse by the blip-bleep of monitors, the jarring lights, the unfamiliarity of the hospital. If we are the ones at the bedside, then we should also be the final guides, the last resort to ease the dying person as they make the transition from life to death. I've sat at a few of those bedsides myself, and I remember the painful disorientation. With each tick of the clock, I wondered what to do. To stay? To go? To speak? To be silent? When my grandfather became ill, I found myself in a state of denial. I thought, surely, he would get better. Surely? If we cannot acknowledge death's approach, we may find that we struggle to provide comfort to the dying; we haven't met them where they are. Facing that hard truth is so painful, and we are so full of fear; it takes great courage both for the dying and the grieving. That is what makes mediators so important.

Years of working with asbestos poisoned my grandfather's lungs, and cancer had already spread to most of his body by the time it was discovered. With such a diagnosis at seventy-two, he couldn't expect much increase to his life expectancy, so he waived chemotherapy treatment and opted for hospice care. Hospices offer care towards improving quality of life until the end of life; they don't work to cure patients, but step in when there is no cure. Hospice care also offers grief support after death, and all of this takes place, usually, in the patient's home.

Hospices operate across the US, UK and mainland Europe: the BBC estimates that there are about 200 hospice clinics in the UK, serving about one-fifth of the population, while the US fares a little better at around two-fifths. Many, like ACCORD Hospice in Renfrewshire, Acorns Children's Hospice in Birmingham, Trinity and St John's in London, are staffed in part by volunteers. These volunteers become death-workers of a different sort, working with nurses and physicians to provide a kind of outreach that – a century ago – the community itself supplied. The hospice workers eased my grandfather's passing, but just as importantly, they eased my grandmother's *mind*. She was losing the only man she'd ever loved, a man who had swept her off her feet as a dashing young sailor home from the war. A whole life with difficulties and struggles, but a life together, was coming to an unceremonious end. And it meant more than words that she – family matriarch, and the one on whom everyone else depended for stability – did not face that end alone. My grandfather did not die a hospital death. He died in his bed, in his home, surrounded by family.

Does that mean the doctor's role at the end of life is obsolete? Not at all. But it does mean something powerfully important: in this modern age, where in the face of death doctors primarily provide palliative services, it falls to the rest of us to provide the *meaning*.

I recently asked a hospice care worker to tell me about this process. In the interest of preserving the confidentiality of her patients, I will refer to her as Jane Carlyle. Jane is the first person that people see at her hospice. She explains the services, answers any questions they have, signs them up if they wish, and dispatches a nurse to assess them for eligibility. Talking about death is still difficult to many, however. 'I believe death is considered taboo because it [the afterlife] is so unknown,' Jane explains. 'We experience death alone and it usually has some pain or suffering involved. Most people are uncomfortable discussing it because it is so personal and it is painful to lose someone.' No one wants to say the wrong thing, Jane explains, so no one says anything. Jane's own family feels too uncomfortable to discuss her work with her, even its most general or humorous aspects. 'It takes a special kind of person,' she explains – and, in fact, it also takes a special kind of training. Jane's hospice provides extensive training to employees and volunteers alike, including classroom training, computer training and at least two months observing fellow nurses, social workers, spiritual care coordinators, volunteers, bereavement staff and doctors. 'What makes a good hospice worker?' I asked. The answer shouldn't surprise us. 'The best hospice workers', Jane said with feeling, 'are those with compassion.' Whether they be nurses or doctors, laypersons or other staff, warmth and the ability to feel with the patient mattered most of all.

'It isn't a job,' Jane explained near the end of our interview. 'It seems to be a calling. I've never seen the calibre of people I work with anywhere else. They are truly invested in the comfort and well-being of each person.' But hospice workers are not superhuman; they face some of the same challenges that resident doctors face. Every patient who enters must be asked the same series of questions, and the experience can become routine. 'Anytime you work with something on a daily basis, it is less shocking and more the norm,' she admitted. But the regularity of the process need not skin over the soft heart with calluses, and in fact, Jane claims some of the most compassionate people she worked with were doctors who saw ageing patients dying all the time. So what does it take to treat the dying with compassion and distance at the same time? I asked Jane to relate her first experience with a dying patient.

Her first 'solo' case was accidental. She arrived at the bedside to find the patient 'actively dying', that is, at the moment of death, but the family did not know it. Death can be so unfamiliar that it arrives under the watchful gaze of loved ones who cannot recognise it, and Jane immediately called for a nurse. The unexpected turn of events meant she faced the room alone, and she admits to feeling wholly unqualified. Something else became apparent, however; this family, this dying patient, were not judges. They felt helpless, and, because Jane was not personally attached to the patient, hers was 'the only clear head in the room'. She gently guided the family through the recognition that death had come, helped to deal with the sudden onset of grief and held a granddaughter's baby so she could say goodbye to her relative. In the meantime, she called the medical supply company about picking up the equipment and finally the funeral home about making arrangements to pick up the body, all before the RN arrived to pronounce the patient dead. Jane called it a privilege to be a part of this family's 'very private, painful moment, and help them through it. That is the best part of what I do.'

Social workers, bereavement staff and spiritual carers listen, counsel and guide. Workers at Jane's hospice follow families for thirteen months after their loved one's death to be sure they are supported through the first anniversary. Hospitals are not generally the best places to die; they can seem too busy or too sterile for comforting reflection at the best of times. But home dying isn't always possible, either, and hospice services can provide another way. The inpatient unit of Jane's hospice care centre is technically similar to a hospital, but she calls it warm and comfortable, with live music playing, food, families and children (and even dogs and cats for pet therapy). People are encouraged to spend time in the kitchen or chapel or down by the lake, and families are accommodated with beds and bathrooms. 'Hospitals are not equipped for this,' Jane reminds me. 'Palliative medicine does make dying better. Let's just forget the tests, outcomes and numbers and concentrate on how you are feeling. [. . .] It makes much more sense to me.'

Awaiting death

'Let's face it, terminal illness does not affect just the patient; it affects the whole family and so many facets of all of their lives.'
—Jane Carlyle

Death comes. Can the West regain what we've lost? Can we cross back over that silent, sterile distance and see death with fresh eyes? Can we make new rituals, forge new paths, try new things – not against the once-pervasive authority of religion and medicine, but *with* them? Home death might be what 70 per cent of Americans want, but even if that is not always possible, there are other ways of finding meaning through new as well as old practices that are gaining or regaining popularity and acceptance. Hospice workers may take patients out on trips, or to parks; one young couple got married on the hospice lawn to answer a dying request. And it isn't only hospice workers making these changes, taking risks. In Washington State, a former forest ranger's dying request was to visit the woodland one last time: hospice workers coordinated with local firefighters to make the transport possible. Perhaps compassion happens best in collaboration – when the hospital doctor recommends his patient to hospice care, when hospice workers reach out to the community to collectively ease the spirits of dying men and women and their families. Death need not be a solo affair. It can be communal, and is perhaps best approached in just that way.

Chapter 7

DEATH COMES
TO DINNER

Getting reacquainted with mortality

You might remember the scene from Monty Python's *The Meaning of Life*; Death interrupts a dinner party to collect souls felled by the salmon mousse. I was eleven or so when I first saw that skit, but it stuck with me. What an odd idea, Death in his robes attending a dinner party. As it turns out, however, this scenario has a long history. In the image below, Death captures a lady diner with his chain. Raphaël Sadeler composed the etching in the sixteenth century, and there are certainly others with a similar theme. From the plague years to the nineteenth century, Death has attended masquerades, dinners, celebrations, drawing rooms and not a few weddings

Death captures a lady with his chain.
Etching by Raphaël Sadeler after Jan van der Straet.

– clearly, he's something of a socialite. In nearly all of this iconography, though, he comes uninvited and unannounced. He throws off his disguise at the most inopportune moment, striking terror into the guests and reminding them that life is fleeting, and pleasure and wealth no refuge. In those etchings and illustrations where Death appears seemingly as an invitee, such as the nineteenth-century print *The Toastmaster* (below) the guests are nonetheless unaware of the danger, and flirt with their doom. Artists and authors used these scenes as a way of warning against intemperate living – and in none of them are we to suppose that the dinner was a healthy one. Surely no one wants Death to meet them for a meal? Perhaps not. Then again, death as a subject has returned to the table with increasing regularity over the last few years, not as a chatter-silencing taboo but as the primary theme. It is the focus of death cafes, death-related Facebook events and death salons – all gaining in popularity. Does this trend represent a return to older notions

The Toastmaster (1816). Coloured aquatint by T. Rowlandson.

of death as a natural part of life? Are we witnessing a shift in death culture, or just another fad, soon to fade?

I began this book with a question: what should we expect when we're expecting death in a culture of opposites – one that chases immortality and disposability with equal fervour? To answer it, we have looked at death practices across cultures and time periods, through the rise (and fall) of Western paternal medical oversight and care. We've investigated the growing gulf between *then* and *now*, the rituals that familiarised the past and the proliferation of options, which has left us in a wilderness of choice. Despite what many say about the desire for choices, when tragedy strikes, most people do not want to wade through a sea of options. We want help, if actual answers are unavailable. We want advisers. We want comfort and support. Sometimes the noise and clatter of competing voices chafes on the raw nerve of our grief. Sometimes silence does the same. Nothing feels right. 'I don't know what to do,' said my friend about the loss of her father. Someone, anyone, *tell me what to do*.

Approaching death: four perspectives

In Chapter Two, we explored four different approaches to grief. Each of these, though unfamiliar to Western eyes, resonates with certain aspects of grief as we in the West experience it: death as transition, grief as rage, 'consuming' grief and the feeling that the dead are still with us. Anthropologists, sociologists and psychologists suggest that grieving is one of the few rites of passage that remains consistent across cultures and times, even if ways of coping with it are wholly different in practice. Science might try to explain *why* we grieve but no one can tell us *how* to grieve in today's world. Just 'knowing' that conflict causes the body to release an inflammation-causing protein – as described in a study by psychologist Janice Kiecolt-Glaser and immunologist Ronald Glaser – or that a loving and familiar touch eases sadness because the brain releases neurotransmitters like oxytocin during 'moments of tenderness', does nothing to support one's actual emotional state during such times. In the midst of deepest sorrow, the brain isn't much help. It's the doing that matters, but the point at which grief descends isn't the time to start 'trying on' different actions or customs suggested by books, television, the internet or well-meaning friends. And sometimes we might know what we ourselves want to do, but struggle to resolve that with the practices of our parents and grandparents: a colleague of mine found herself at the centre of a family feud over the last wishes of her father, an atheist, and unsure how to approach her devoutly Catholic family. Ritual should be like a familiar touch, something safe, something that gives comfort – not a sticking point that opens fresh wounds. How can we arrive at this safe place? It isn't easy. But seeking comfort is right and good. If anything, this is our most natural response, and finding ways to progress through grief, even when we may not agree on everything, is very important.

Comfort may lie in a caress, an embrace, a shared meal, a common ground. But there is another kind of comfort, just as important: during times of deep grief, we also seek *meaning*, and many of our historical rituals existed to provide (or emphasise) precisely that. What is the meaning of death? What is the meaning of life – of this life – of all life? These are not idle questions. In all cultures and at all times, humans have asked and sought and hoped.

Sometimes the best comfort can come from knowing you are not alone in your grief – that others have felt as you do, whether you find them through support groups, literature or in your own existing circle. To know this is not to gain comfort by removing the ache, but to help us to feel less alone in the midst of aching. Rose Kennedy, mother of President John F. Kennedy, put it this way: 'It has been said, "time heals all wounds." I do not agree. The wounds remain. In time, the mind, protecting its sanity, covers them with scar tissue and the pain lessens. But it is never gone.'

The best we can do is the best we can do – and whether you subscribe to Kübler-Ross's five stages or a journey of a thousand steps, the process varies with each person, with each death. In earlier chapters, we looked at death from the perspective of different cultures and times past. Let's now look at those death practices that are closer to home and the here and now, wherever they may have first begun. How do we do things today in the US and the UK and other parts of Western Europe? Are traditions disappearing? Or just evolving? And in what ways are we influenced by other traditions from other cultures now practised within our countries? As I mentioned earlier: despite the intensity of our solitude during grief, we are never alone in suffering.

The funeral

For many, funerals remain the most recognisable and expected form of death practice. What, then, is the value of the funeral? In the terrible aftermath of the Malaysian Airlines Flight M-17 crash of July 2014, families in nine countries began the agonising wait for the bodies of their loved ones to be recovered. Having been shot down in rebel territory between Russia and Ukraine, the flight's remains were scattered over highly danger-ous ground. The limited access and slow recovery recalled the disappearance of another Malaysian Airlines aircraft, Flight 370, over the ocean earlier in 2014. At the time of writing, many who lost loved ones in these disasters still had no graves at which to mourn. Specific burial rites such as those practised by Islamic Malaysians (many of whom were on board both flights) require burial on the day of death. In response, the Fatwa Council, Malaysia's highest Muslim body, refused to declare Flight 370 passengers dead. This solved the problem of death ritual, but introduced new ones – such as difficulties in collecting life insurance, and all the other legal hurdles that attend the fam-ilies of the missing. The *Wall Street Journal* quoted the wife of a missing passenger as saying 'Our [plane] is still missing. How to move on?' Similar questions are asked by the relatives of people who go missing in other ways. In June 2009, Australian parents Suzanne Wallace and Bruce Herbert lost their adult son Andrew; five years later, they want to perform a bodiless burial, though they admit, 'without Andrew's body, I don't think we will ever get closure. We can't move forward.' The body is material. What we do with it, when, and how, matters.

The US is home to many ethnic and cultural groups. You might say that the nation was built of immigrants, since apart from indigenous tribes, absolutely everyone else arrived from abroad at some point. Most people from the US are taught that 'America' is a 'melting pot' – despite the fact that the name 'America' covers North and South and Central America, or that the metaphor glosses over bloody battles and the oppression of numerous people and groups. A more appropriate depiction comes from Colin Woodard in his book *American Nations*; he looks at regionalism, and describes eleven smaller 'nations' within the US's broad borders. And yet, funerals in the US remain remarkably similar regardless of where in the country they take place.

In most cases, bodies are taken by a funeral home, embalmed and prepared for viewing, as those in the US frequently opt for open caskets. After the viewing (also held at the funeral home in most cases) comes the service. This may be secular or religious, but in the great proportion of cases, it, too, takes place at the same location, and may be arranged by funeral staff rather than the clergy. It's a somewhat surprising statistic, given that 70 per cent of US citizens still identify as Christians (and about 20 per cent of them as Catholics). Even so, while weddings may take place in churches even when the parties involved are no longer believers, even believers tend to hold funerals in funeral homes rather than at church. This is worthy of an additional comment: in the US, there is separation of church and state, meaning that if you choose to be married by a religious authority you must first and foremost obtain a marriage licence. This can seem slightly incongruous to outsiders, but because of that separation of church and state, the US is technically a secular country, albeit one with a lot of religious people in it. Marriage laws differ depending on the state, but as an example, authorisation to solemnise marriages in Ohio is issued by the Secretary of State's office to any ordained or licensed minister requesting the licence. Of course, you can also obtain your own from the courthouse in advance of the marriage ceremony (I did), meaning that the ceremony may be essentially just that: *a ceremony*. The ritual process of getting married remains incredibly important, however; people plan their weddings far in advance and down to the last detail. This is not widely the case for the funeral. Frequently, much of the arrangement for this final event of life falls to the funeral home officiates, shortly before the funeral takes place.

In a national study of American morticians, V. R. Pine discovered that in a nation of roughly 200 million, 50,000 licensed funeral directors operate 22,000 funeral establishments and together take care of nearly all the dead in the US. Embalming has become the universally accepted practice, even though not required by law, and even though it merely slows the body's deterioration. Most funerals are conducted directly from a funeral home regardless of religious affiliation, and 92 per cent of all deaths result in earth-burial. Cremation, which is less popular in the US than in Europe, only takes place in 4 per cent of deaths annually. Though it spans so many cultures, creeds and customs, the US funeral industry treats bodies almost exactly the same way from coast to coast, with the funeral 'director' (possibly a better title than mortician, considering their scope of activity) presiding over the corpse from its arrival, through its embalming and preparation, to the choice of coffin, the viewing, the service and the burial.

In my youth I was puzzled by the embalming practice, and for me it still seems the strangest part of the process. For one thing, preservation isn't complete; unlike the Egyptian interment of the dead, where the bodies are truly preserved, embalming only stops decay for a matter of weeks. What is its purpose, then? As I mentioned in Chapter One, it began after the Civil War so that dead soldiers might still be recognised by the families they'd be returned to, and in a way, that idea lingers. Embalming prevents mourners from confronting death head-on by maintaining skin colour (through dyed embalming fluid) and other aspects of lifelikeness. In Britain, where open coffins and public viewing of the corpse are not standard and cremation is more common, mourners may not see the dead body at any stage of the process, which suggests a similar denial or glossing-over of the reality of death. So why continue with embalming – or any of the other before-burial preparations – today, when circumstances are so different? The rites associated with funerals are socially prescribed: the 'proper' ways of dealing with the dead. In many respects the embalming, the flowers and even the casket serve no practical purpose.

The truth is, most of us just never ask why. It takes something unusual breaking in from outside to make us see the constructed nature of the typical funeral and the incongruity surrounding our treatment of the dead. Funerals, in their sameness, provide a framework for mourners. Funeral directors, meanwhile, provide the stability that once came from religious or medical figures.

The tightly organised funeral industry controls everything that happens to our bodies once we die, which makes their trade both lucrative and consistent. In 1963 Jessica Mitford, in her groundbreaking book *The American Way of Death,* attacked the industry and directors for precisely this level of control, claiming they were motivated by rampant capitalism and maintained by exploitation. The industry, she claimed, 'sells' rituals to grieving families – and they are very costly. Her exposé launched a consumer movement that resulted in changes and improved regulation, but throughout much of the book, she also ruthlessly denigrates ritual practice itself. Her social harangue targets not only funerals but also mourners, casting them as irrational and gullible. Theology professor Thomas Long worried that, as a direct result of Mitford's work, Americans were 'in danger of losing the capacity to mark ritually the profound significance of the experience of death'. That fear has proven groundless in at least one important way; today the grief-stricken may struggle for a foothold in the void, but funerals have remained, in themselves, the primary ritual of death in the US.

Is it fair to ask whether funeral directors have taken on too much control over the process? Was Mitford right in attacking the industry? She has not been the only one; in August of 2013 an anonymous writer who identified as a funeral director provided his or her own exposé, claiming that 'this isn't a hospital and I don't provide a service – this is a business'. Whether this piece was truly written by a funeral director or by a disgruntled 'customer', the point remains the same: not everyone is happy with the ubiquity of the funeral industry. So – especially given the push towards autonomy and choice in the medical industry – why are so many Americans so willing to give over the planning and process to a third party when it comes to death?

It might be easier to understand this by considering what services are, in fact, offered – broadening the perspective to include the United Kingdom. In the UK, a mortuary licence isn't necessary for funeral directors, though the British Institute of Funeral Directors (BIFD) offers a Licence to Practise to professionals who follow the Institute's requirements for annual 'Continuous Professional Development'. The National Association of Funeral Directors includes 3,200 funeral homes in the UK, the broadest membership of any mortuary association. An NAFD director, like his or her US counterpart, arranges nearly all of the events and practices associated with death and burial, including scheduling the date and time with the church if there is one, the cemetery or the crematorium, and all paperwork. In addition, they will:

Transfer the deceased from the place of death
Offer a choice of coffins and caskets to 'suit a range of
    budgets and individual choice'
Provide facilities for viewing prior to the funeral
Provide the necessary vehicles and staff to conduct the
    funeral with 'dignity and professionalism'
Place death notices
Arrange for catering
Arrange special musical requests
Make arrangements for the subsequent disposal of the
    remains

Order and care for flowers, or arrange for donations
Supply obituary cards or thank you cards

Not surprisingly, both American and British services can be pricey, and along with these other services, directors usually provide information on how to arrange for payment; some even offer payment plans. Historically, this was even more important – the shame of not being able to afford a 'good' funeral was often considered too much to bear (a sentiment that is echoed in other cultures; remember that the Indonesian Torajans spend more time and money on a funeral than a wedding). The extensive service packages of the funeral directors may seem all-encompassing, but they mean that those in mourning need not make any decision alone. And that has its advantages.

One evening in March 2002, my grandmother laid out the quilt she intended me to inherit. She set out several other items, too, including her Bible, which lay open on the foot-stool. She called her family members, including an estranged brother in Arizona, and then she went to bed. She never woke up. During the night, her heart – strained by a congestive condition – simply ceased to beat. My mother and father discovered her, still lying peacefully in bed. It's the end most of us wish for. Quiet. Painless. Seemingly prepared for. But to those of us remaining, her death was still a terrible, painful shock, a rending of the synapses that may as well have been the tearing of connective tissue. She had outlived my grandfather by seven years. Now she was gone, and we were left adrift, but there was no time to sit and contemplate: we had to respond to the seemingly endless list of things that have to be done when someone dies. Regardless of where you live, numerous people have to be notified, and the checklist can be substantial – a number of websites carefully explain procedures and responsibilities to avoid confusion. French law, for example, requires that a funeral take place within a minimum of twenty-four hours and a maximum of six days, and most of it must be authorised by the mayor of the town or city where the death occurs. The legal responsibility of declaring the death also resides with the family, and must be reported to the town hall (*la mairie*). The same is true in Britain, where you must register a death just as you would register a birth, and in the US.

But when we lost my grandmother, our first call was to the funeral home. Why? Following a death in a hospital, the doctor will usually provide a death certificate. However, when someone has died at home of natural causes, as both my grandparents did, the funeral director can provide practical assistance, including completing and filing death certificate paperwork. The director's role thus begins before the funeral, which can be a great comfort during the time of bereavement. In my grandmother's case, the funeral home received her body and began the practical preparations before I arrived back in town to help. Chaos seemed to be erupting all around us – my parents owned a business and my grandmother was part owner and a third of the staff; there were relatives to inform and a hundred other small tasks. We were only too happy to have the other death details worked out on our behalf.

The cleaning of my grandmother's house fell to me. Things needed to be put in order; she wouldn't have wanted anyone to see it a mess, my mother told me, and I agreed. It's the small things, sometimes, isn't it? That someone who knew and loved her should tidy the kitchen: this was deeply meaningful to us. At the time, I was the only one able to enter without breaking down – though in the privacy of her house, I wept more openly than I would normally do. I remember finding my wedding bouquet from two years earlier; she had carefully preserved it for me, and I thought how oddly similar the rituals for marrying and for burying were. I had intended to keep this token, but in the depth of sorrow, I could scarcely look at it. I let it be taken away with other things, and even now, that's a bit painful to relate.

Seven years earlier, I'd sat at my grandfather's wake, a confused teenager. Now, it was I who went with my mother and uncles to the funeral home. There would be two funerals, one in Ohio and one in West Virginia. The logistics would have been maddening had we faced them alone, but we didn't. We sat in comfortable chairs in a room with vaguely Victorian decor while the director spoke to us about options. His eyes flitted back to me often, and I knew why. My mother was in charge of the necessaries, but of the four of us, I had the most visible composure. He took us down to show us coffins; I recall my uncle requesting 'the best', something white – 'she loved lilies'. In the US, you have a legal right to bring your own coffin to a funeral home, but who owns a coffin? Not many people – nor do most want to spend time searching for alternative suppliers at this stage. So we chose one, and then left the director and morticians to dress and prepare my grandmother for the viewing.

Exhausted, unsteady, uncertain, we piled back into the car

and drove home through the rain. I had no idea what would be happening in that little room, and I did not want to know. I was only too happy that someone, anyone, could tell me what to do. After the funeral, though, I remember thinking that somehow my grandfather's burial had been more meaningful. Perhaps not having my cousin there to do the service made it seem more impersonal this time. But somehow, the grief felt deeper, and I wished we could have done other, better, more. Why is it that so often with death we blindly follow certain patterns when, in fact, there are other options available, if we only looked for them? Because for most of us, we simply *have not thought about it*. Unlike wedding planning, in which our loved ones tend to enthusiastically take part (or at least begrudgingly tolerate), death planning seems too dark, too dismal, too unreal to be brought up as a subject. When is a good time, after all? But some things are worth talking about, and there are choices worth considering.

Green burial: natural death in a new light

My first introduction to the concept of 'natural death' came through the Natural Death Centre's handbook, edited by Rupert Callender. My friend and fellow historian Richard Barnett wrote a short piece called 'The Sense of an Ending: A Brief History of Modern Death' for one of three little volumes that make up the *Natural Death Handbook*'s fifth edition. Called simply *Writings on Death*, the slim book provided essays, poems and reflections, what Callender describes as 'smoked glass, through which together we might glimpse death's outline'. I emailed Richard immediately – 'Do you think I might review a copy?' I asked, and the box, cloth-covered and tied in blue ribbon, arrived in the post some days later. I had never encountered anything like it.

The handbook, the largest of the three-piece set, speaks with simple clarity and grace about the best practices in the UK for *dealing with the body yourself*. No funeral home necessary: the pages explain sitting with the dying, washing and cooling a loved one after passing, and preparing the body for a natural funeral. In its quiet, considerate and measured tone, the handbook offers gentle advice from chapter to chapter and ends, appropriately, with the grieving process itself once the earth has been turned. Appearing throughout are personal stories and testimonies, the practical experience of those who chose the natural death method and the quiet serenity of home wakes and preparations (and their practical considerations). Also included? A directory of natural death sites and accommodating funeral directors in the UK.

Since then, I've learned of many natural death funerals and funerary services. In Germany the dying can opt for woodland burial, with about forty burial sites in the German countryside. New Zealand, Australia, Canada, Italy, Ireland and the Netherlands have natural burial sites (though French law prohibits them). Jeff Jorgenson works as managing owner of Elemental, a 'green' burial service in Seattle, US. Jeff, a mortician, felt that funeral homes retained too much control of arrangements and didn't always allow families to be part of important decisions. In addition, he wanted to offer services for those concerned about the environment; Elemental attempts to reduce waste, take part in habitat restoration and source locally. The *San Francisco Gate* reported in 2013 that 'green burial' restores and preserves the land, potentially reducing the environmental impact of a society of ageing baby boomers. The practice has caught on in the American Midwest, too, and the Foxfield Preserve of Ohio provides an alternative that helps protect land while providing funding for nature education and conservation. They claim to offer families peace and even a sense of meaning – a meaningful goodbye.

How does practice provide meaning? It depends on who is practising. Because the natural death movement tends to engage families in the choices and practices surrounding death (including the hopes and ideals of the dying), they participate in meaning-making. Remember the Cambodians who created a new ritual to replace those lost during the Pol Pot period: if ritual is part of healing, and we are part of the ritual, *we* are part of the healing.

The editors of the *Natural Death Handbook* explain that, in many ways, the natural death movement is a secular one. However, it is not exclusively secular, just as ours is not an exclusively secular world. In fact, death is where our distinctions between science, self and sanctity most often break down. A funeral may not be held under the auspices of a particular church (or even a particular god), but spiritual healing and comfort are not necessarily eschewed. The best part of the natural death movement comes, I think, from its flexibility and the encouragement to think in advance about what it is our loved ones (and ourselves) would like. But it's also the best time to think about other aspects of death and dying; for instance, what about organ donation? Mary Roach talks at length about this in *Stiff*; if we are willing to submit to medical intervention to save our own lives, what about the lives of others when we are gone? Roach also asks whether it makes sense to 'try to control what happens to your remains when you are no longer around to reap the joys or benefits of that control'. The answer to both concerns, of donation and of the kind of service, depends entirely on the individual, his or her family context, culture and expectations. The question might reasonably be rephrased to reflect what I've said in earlier chapters: death is communal, a community event – shouldn't other people be involved as we plan for death, just as we plan for other major events in our lives? Whether an individual opts for a funeral home, a church or one of the natural sites appearing around the country, each of us ought to aim for this building up to the event, a shared meaning-making that helps to heal us and draw us together.

We all feel death's sting and separation keenly. If death of a loved one is a wound, even an amputation, let us seek ways of binding together rather than allowing grief to isolate and pull us asunder. New means of doing this are cropping up in exactly this way, with some opting for parties and celebrations at the graveside, others choosing to be buried in unusually shaped coffins (from Cadillacs to decorated coffins that are, in themselves, works of art). Pia Interlandi, a fashion designer from Melbourne, creates biodegradable 'Garments for the Grave' in consultation with the living (that is, her creations are 'bespoke' by the dying, often long before death). In her article 'After Death: 8 Burial Alternatives That Are Going Mainstream', Stephanie Pappas mentions 'eternal reefs', places where concrete orbs of human remains help to expand or rebuild coral reef areas. Death takes; ritual remakes. Death and memorial may be as varied as we are. And so it should be.

The memorial and the media

I am convinced that it is not the fear of death, of our lives
ending that haunts our sleep so much as the fear . . . that as
far as the world is concerned, we might as well never have lived.
—Rabbi Harold Kushner

In Chapter One, I described the difference between death as event and as process. The process of dying – including the time before and after the death – is one that involves the living, and the funeral, in whatever form, only marks the beginning. It just isn't enough by itself. Not long ago, the British television personality Kirstie Allsopp spoke to the *Telegraph* about her mother's death. 'We don't get it right in this country,' she said, 'we may get it more wrong than any other country in the entire world.' The problem isn't necessarily the kind of funeral that takes place, but all that happens (or doesn't happen) after it. After the funeral, 'We are supposed to move on, except of course we can't. It's a slammed door which you cannot reopen, and it's a huge door. So we do get it wrong. We don't have the traditions in place. Whatever the traditions are in other faiths, they're better.' While this sentiment might represent some of that too-near-association I spoke of earlier – the familiarity that causes us to think our own practices aren't meaningful or helpful – it also speaks to a wider fear that the conventional process of mourning, culminating in the funeral, aren't providing what people in the UK most need. How might they be adjusted, and so reinvigorated?

The greatest part of mourning really happens after the last cold clod of earth has been cast over the grave or the coffin sent to the cremation chamber; after the guests go home and back to their lives; after the silent car rolls down the silent driveway and you find yourself in the fuzzy dark of a long ever-after. The dead have gone, we remain and we *remember*. Grieving revolves around memory and memorial; from the preserved ringlets of hair to the memento mori photograph, we long to 'keep' the dead with us in some meaningful way. The height of that tradition may have passed with the Victorian age, but we humans rarely leave anything entirely behind. In June of 2014, one American family made headlines for posing their deceased mother as though alive for her viewing. Surrounded by her favourite things, Miriam Burbank 'attended' her own funeral in New Orleans with a can of beer, a cigarette and a disco ball. Even more disturbing to some, the late boxer Christopher Rivera posed standing, as though entering the ring one last time, for his wake. Some found these arrangements tasteless and tacky – but we know better. Miriam and Christopher joined a long tradition of preserving life-in-death, a way of keeping the 'dead with us' that seems uncanny only because in today's world we've separated life and death so completely.

Or have we? Candi Cann is an assistant professor at Baylor University, Texas, researching death, dying and the impact of remembering. Referencing memorial tattoos, car decals and the mobile memorials (including public shrines of flowers, candles, soft toys and messages) that appear after tragedies, Cann explains that 'when bereavement is no longer given public space in society or culture, people must create and adopt alternative forms of mourning to help them navigate public space with their altered status as grieving individuals'. In other words, we seek ways of speaking and sharing our grief, not unlike the Victorians in their black crape and memorial jewellery. Some of the tattoos, Cann explains, go a step further. By mixing the cremated remains into the ink and then having the ink transferred into their very skin, mourners can wear the body of the dead – a memorial of incorporation that seems more similar to the death-consumption practices of the Wari than of the Victorian memorial brooch. The dead live on in the living, making a home in the light and warmth of those who remain rather than being interred in the earth somewhere far away.

Memorials like this honour the material of the physical body – the fabric of ourselves. But ours is a digital age, and increasingly we lead hybrid lives of wireless connections, Facebook friends and expanding networks of people we may rarely if ever meet. Internet memorials sit alongside physical tributes but, even more than a tattoo, give us constant accessibility. But it's worth asking: is this a good thing? Researcher Dennis Draeger has described the fears faced by family members about monitoring, preserving or protecting a deceased loved one's online activity. I was curious; how important might that be? As it turns out, Facebook alone has 30 million accounts set as 'deceased', and as these profiles become memorialised they are subject to new privacy policies. 'What happens', Draeger asks, 'to the currency left in online accounts when passwords are not designated to the deceased's heirs? Conversely, who can view the skeletons – of the deceased, or their contacts' skeletons shared in private messages – locked in digital closets when those passwords are found? Who owns the data left behind, and who has the power to decide how it is used?' The solutions to these problems can be equally unsettling; the Facebook app 'If I Die' posthumously posts messages to friends on certain dates – even after a profile has been designated deceased.

In June of 2014, *The Atlantic* carried a story by Julie Buntin called 'She's Still Dying on Facebook'. In it, Buntin describes the strange grief journey that digital permanence provides. Lea, formerly her best friend, died of substance-abuse-related liver failure. But, Buntin claims, she died more than once – she 'died digitally' first (in the sense that her activity declined on Facebook, then stopped altogether); then actually; and in incremental ways, she *still* dies. 'I'm dogged by our messages [. . .] In some ways, it's worse that Facebook is almost all I have of her,' Buntin explains, unable to reconcile her 'anger at Lea's Facebook for posing as her living self, for tricking me, momentarily, into believing that if I post I will somehow reach her.' Memento mori photographs, in their stasis, allow for some reinterpretation; and yet, the strange half-life of a Facebook memorial creates for Buntin a cycle of endless mourning.

When I first read Buntin's story, I felt a combined sense of

horror and of fellow-feeling. The question of digital memo-
rialisation came up once before for me, at a lecture I gave for
the Museum of Contemporary Art in Cleveland. Part of the
Dirge: Reflections on Life and Death series, my talk was called
'Draw Nigh: Approaching Death in a Culture of Immortality'.
It was pouring rain, cold for spring and the crowd rather intimate in size. Perhaps because of that, the audience participated
in a lively Q&A. One young woman raised her hand and asked
if I considered online memorials to be 'like' memento mori
photography. Were we just the same as the Victorians? (It's a
loaded question – I'm a historian, after all, and believe just
about everything repeats itself.) When I asked for clarification,
she talked about the Facebook memorials – slightly scandal-
ising some of the other audience members who had yet to
hear of such a thing. 'You're kidding! Is that legal?' someone
asked – and I can understand why. I shudder to think of all the
nonsense I've posted over the years on social media; imagining
it freeze-framed, cut off in the middle and solidified, slightly
terrifies me. I am not my Facebook profile. I am not my Twitter
feed, either – or my LinkedIn, Spoke or Goodreads pages. I'm
not even my blog or website. Would I want these to be the
final representations of a life lived? Such questions were once
reserved for celebrities of stage and screen, whose likenesses
would long outlive them, their youthful visages gracing old
film in endless loops. Now we are all potentially haunted by the
ghosts of our past selves, and it's more than just dust swirling
in sunlit windows.

'In some ways, I think it's very like,' I answered. And I still
do. The memorial mediums have changed, but the impulses are

the same. We want to keep a piece of the dead with us. And yet, in other ways, memorials of this kind – due to the magic of technology and its ability to preserve, if not wholly to animate, the dead – seem less like us holding onto the dead, and more like the dead holding onto us. The Torajans celebrate the dead because the dead can influence the living. They have power of a kind. This is true of the Bolivian household skulls as well. The memorialising partly assuages grief, for they suggest that the dead have not truly gone. Or at the very least, that they haven't gone *far*.

The immortality provided by algorithms can't approximate a personality yet, but we make greater strides every year in that direction. Draeger asks whether we'll see a resurgence of ancestor worship; that is, will we continue to visit the shrines of the now-deceased on Facebook or other media, consulting them, asking their advice? Stranger still, as he goes on to say, 'will we begin to see a new emotion arise – one of mourning for a loved one mixed with joy and affection toward a machine housing that loved one's digital resurrection?' It might seem improbable, but psychologists take such things seriously. Many suggest that mourning periods will extend as a result, lasting perhaps for years. Once again, though, the Victorians did that long before us.

Social media memorials may not offer anything new, after all. What they can do, perhaps, is open a window onto something old – the sense that boundaries between life and death are permeable, and that grief, like a deep-water beast, reveals itself only in pieces. Submerged for a while, now the head appears, now a tail, breaking the surface of our lives with a sudden crest of fresh feeling. No memorial has ever truly been static; even those daguerreotype photos, so pristinely locked between silver plate and glass, would have taken on new meaning as time changed the mourner's relationship to their reality. I still miss my grandmother and grandfather, but their faces and voices, the sound of their laughter, the very words they spoke, have changed. I remember them very well, but older eyes see differently. I recall the best things. I forget the painful things. I don't remember their faded forms, ill and tired near the end. I remember them robust. The digital might seem to offer us more permanence, but the fragmented, partial nature of online profiles, frozen in time, may be painful. On the other hand, memorials that we build, not those preserved by the vagaries of algorithms and the misfortune of timing, give us a chance to reinvent and celebrate. The standing boxer, the mother with her cigarette, can offer us something: perspective. How we see affects what we see, and seeing, as the anatomist would say, is believing.

Salon and story

The funeral and the process of grief may be the most powerful of our introductions to death, but they aren't the only means of approach. I said earlier that 'knowing' does not help us much through the pain and anguish of deep mourning. And yet, we seek to know – and that knowing itself offers a kind of power. What, in your own life, first gave you the shadowed outline of mortality? The death of a pet, perhaps? The discovery of an injured and dying baby bird in the back garden? My youthful question about the tenure of 'forever' gets at the heart of the matter: we feel grief, but can we really *know* death? If so, what kind of knowledge is it and how do we come by it?

In 2013, I attended the first Death Salon as a participant and co-organiser. This usually takes a bit of explaining, as it conjures images of gothic hair studios for some. Salon, in this sense, refers to the eighteenth-century practice of gathering for intellectual discussion in private homes, usually in the 'salon' or drawing room. This particular salon brings together 'intellectuals and independent thinkers engaged in the exploration of our shared mortality' through engagement with art, history and much more. This aspect of Death Salon is its most laudable; it provides a place where the curious as well as the informed can meet and discuss mortal concerns. The first Salon featured brilliant speakers on diverse topics; Caitlin Doughty (of the YouTube series *Ask a Mortician*, Order of the Good Death, and author of *Smoke Gets in Your Eyes*) curated the first day, including the round-table about gender and mortality that I took part in. Morbid Anatomy Library (Joanna Ebenstein) curated day two, and between these events was the 'Death Cabaret', part celebration, part conference 'lightning talks'. Many people I've mentioned in this book took part, including Lindsey Fitzharris, Bess Lovejoy, Jeff Jorgenson and Paul Koudounaris. Considered part of the 'death-positive' movement, the Salon intends, as the website directs, to break the taboo surrounding an overly sanitised culture of death.

But these aims, lauded in an article called 'Death is Having a Moment' by Erika Hayasaki, do not garner universal acclaim.

Shortly after the Salon ended, a comment posted to Hayasaki's *Atlantic* piece proclaimed that '[t]his death poetry, death salons, is just a self-deluding fantasy of upper-class twits, who are still healthy, privileged and protected, and who know very little about real life'. The author apologised a few threads later, but at the core of the critique is a question. When Death comes to dinner, do those who have yet to experience death, dying, ageing or tragedy have a place at the table?

When we experience tragedy, we rarely want to speak or listen to those who have not witnessed its wreckage in their own lives. I remember how hollow the words of comfort sounded from people I *knew* could not understand – and in the rage of my grief I wanted to order them all to be silent. Of course, silence can be just as bad; anything is apt to feel painful when your nerves are that raw. Such responses may be born out of private pain, but that doesn't make them fair. In what other aspect of life would we exclude the willing learner from greater knowledge based solely on their inexperience? The 'healthy, privileged and protected' make up precisely that group for whom death comes unexpectedly, catching them unawares. Among them are the medical interns, the young doctors and all those who – because young and/or lucky – have thus far avoided coming too close to death.

The director and founder of Death Salon, Megan Rosenbloom, coordinated the inaugural meeting so that we might attend a talk given by author Mary Roach. Roach speaks eloquently about subjects as diverse (and taboo) as sex, death and digestion. Lively and engaging, she makes the unfamiliar familiar. At the end of that evening's event, Death Salon attendees gathered, and I found myself in a group of young women, all rather a lot younger than myself. Given our evening and the conference ahead, the natural question arose: what brings you to Death Salon? While answering, I mentioned my early acquaintance with mortality and my experience having witnessed death first-hand. I hadn't intended this to be surprising, and in fact used it mainly as context. And yet it was met with surprise, and even a kind of fleeting awe. Though the conference attendees ranged from morticians to academics, a proportion of our group had come, quite literally, to learn about death – because they had no experience of it in their own lives. What was it like, they wanted to know? What can we expect?

The hunger for knowledge and the search for meaning in death may seem like the morbid musings of those who have nothing better to do – or like the only things worth pursuing at all. The difficulty of contemplating death and dying lies in their resistance to easy answers and textbook classifications. I'm honoured that anyone might ask me what to expect about dying, but truthfully, I can only offer my own experiences and speculation.

Less than a year after Death Salon LA, a friend asked me a question that (somewhat surprisingly) hadn't come up at the conference. Did I, he wondered, fear death? It's a ponderous question. 'No,' I said, after some thought. 'I don't.' What was the secret, then? Religion? Knowledge? More conferences? We talked for an hour, not so I could lay out my methods but so I could convince him that *there is no secret*, no way of approaching death that is right, no way of assuaging fears and frustrations. Today, I do not fear death. Ask me tomorrow; ask me when I'm faced with the illness of a loved one, ask me when I come face to face with my own mortality. But by all means, keep asking. That's what we have – and this compendium of shared knowledge makes up all we can achieve intellectually. To go deeper requires nearer experience, and that will come with time, whether we want it or not. In the meantime, we should endeavour by whatever means possible to keep talking. Storytelling remains the one thing that so many other cultural traditions have in common. The story of the Tibetan wheel of life, reincarnation and the 'living Buddhas'; the story of other-worldly influence represented by the *famadihana* offerings in Madagascar or the household skulls of Bolivia; the consumption of the dead for the Wari or the nourishing of the dead for Torajans – in all of these traditions, death requires talk, and death talk requires care and feeding.

Strange dining companions

I began this chapter by asking who among us would invite Death to dinner? In most cultures, in most time periods, humans have used mealtimes as a means of reinforcing bonds, sharing cultural knowledge and otherwise providing comfort and succour. It's no wonder food takes on such significance or that it makes up part of humanity's most profound rituals. What wedding doesn't end in a feast? Even the arrival of new life brings with it food customs; I lived in a small Minnesota town for a few years, and whenever a baby arrived the community pitched in to cook meals for the new parents. At the other end of life's spectrum we have the funeral feasts, ritual dining and 'comfort' food that accompany death. Sarah Troop, curator of the Lindsay Museum, host of the *Cabinet of Curiosities* podcasts and the editor of *Nourishing Death*, a blog dedicated to funeral food, suggests that food has primarily been used in three different ways as it relates to death: for mourners, for feeding the dead or the dying or to nourish the earth itself. Dr Christina Lee, author of *Feasting the Dead*, talks about how important funeral food was to early Anglo-Saxons, and I have here examined the feasts of other cultural traditions surrounding death.

Even the cycle of harvests providing the goods offers up a remembrance of life and death: the dying seed, the germination of crops and finally the harvest. In our world of modern conveniences, where food has been so divorced from its roots that we can scarcely see the resemblance between the pig and the bacon, the cow and the plastic jug of homogenised milk, some of those connections have been lost. Lurid but true examples abound. My parents owned a small grocery and deli counter for some years, and during the mad-cow scare, they worried over the price and availability of meat and milk. One customer scoffed at their anxiety, saying, 'I never worry about cows; I get my milk from the supermarket!' Even so, we have retained some of the food rituals of our forebears – and in the northern hemisphere, many still partake of a midwinter feast, regardless of religious persuasion. These meals began as a way of consuming the best of the harvest before it could spoil, and as a means of fattening up for the lean months between midwinter and the thaw. Struggling subsistence farmers understood very well the relationship between food and death, the having and the not having, as do so many impoverished people today. So death and dinner have a lot of common ground, and yet, inheriting the *politesse* of the eighteenth and nineteenth centuries, perhaps, we rarely bring up mortality at such times. You can almost imagine the response – *you can't talk about that now, I'm eating!*

That is precisely the point of a new kind of dining engagement: dates with death. Organisations have recently popped up across the US, including one that began (not surprisingly) with a conversation. Michael Hebb met two doctors on a train who told him that 50 per cent of Americans don't die as they hope or intend to. Hebb decided to get the death conversation started among family and friends. The initial idea, *Let's Have Dinner and Talk about Death*, began in 1997 and grew to become a collaborative series of events now known as Death Over Dinner. The website helps users to plan, and recommends reading about grief and at least one audio or video (of the user's choice). Finally, a packet of information is sent with suggested language for invites, and after the event, all are encouraged to share their stories. As the site presents it: 'How we want to die represents the most important and costly conversation America isn't having.'

Much of the UK, as Kirstie Allsopp attests, isn't having it either. Or, at least, it *wasn't*. The *Daily Mail* picked up the story of death dinners in September 2013, noting that despite its American roots, Death Over Dinner now has listings in the UK, Australia and Canada. Jon Underwood created the Death Cafe, based on a Swiss concept, and what started as a conversation has become a movement in London and beyond, spreading across the globe. In 2013, America's National Public Radio covered the story, quoting Underwood, who described a tradition in continental Europe of meeting in public (rather than the private salon) to discuss important subjects. 'There's a *café philo*, which is a philosophical cafe,' he explained, 'and a *café scientifique*. And Bernard Crettaz, he's a Swiss sociologist, set up a *café mortel*, or death cafe.' Why not bring that tradition to others – particularly in the UK and the US, where such conversations don't appear to be happening otherwise?

Who would invite Death to dinner? An awful lot of folks, as it turns out – not because they are seeking out morbid matters or courting their own mortality, but because they are curious, hurting, estranged and in need. In a 2014 article for the *Guardian*, Eleanor Tucker describes her first Death Cafe experience in Edinburgh. Her host, Rebecca Newbigging, explained, 'Talking about it can only be a good thing: not only does coming to terms with your own mortality mean you're more likely to live life to the full, being open about it means we can support each other, our families and ourselves when death has an impact on our lives.'

Tucker, whose sister is a doctor working in palliative care, agreed with Newbigging's sentiment. Describing the disbelief felt by family members when told a loved one will die, Tucker asks: 'How have we got to the stage in our sanitised society where we can't bring ourselves to believe anyone is going to die?' This recalls the paradox of our modern world, the tension between immortality and disposability. Perhaps they are the same thing, in a way; disposable means replaceable, and we're seduced by the promise of immortality based on replacement parts. Why shouldn't we be able to retrofit indefinitely, rebuilding our engines to carry us into that uncertain future? But the myth of physical immortality collapses when the curtain falls for the last time, and as Michael DeGeorgia and many other doctors can attest, neither the family nor the doctor are ever really quite prepared for it. Death cafes do not offer support for the grieving in the sense of counselling. Anyone is welcome to attend – whether they have experienced a death or not – and the conversation is not a grief support group. In fact, their events may not, they suggest, be appropriate for the recently bereaved, who may not be ready to talk to strangers about death in the abstract. In addition, because these events are run by individuals with an interest and not a speciality, the Death Cafe cannot provide the kind of aid that a counsellor or therapist can. But this doesn't mean the events aren't helpful, thought-provoking and deeply moving. Telling the story – sharing the knowledge of death – over coffee and tea revisits the old storytelling means of transferring cultural knowledge.

One criticism of the cafes, rather like the comment levelled at Death Salon, takes aim at the number of young people in attendance. The numbers tell a different story, however. The median age might surprise those who think only the young and healthy show up – it certainly surprises first-time attendees. Katelyn Verstraten, a reporter for *The Star* in Toronto, assumed she would be surrounded by goths, drinking coffee in crypts and talking about ghosts. Instead, she found herself 'directed upstairs to a bright, sunny room at the cemetery's visitation centre' amid soothing music and a mix of young people and senior citizens. The largest constituent of the death dinners operates somewhere in the middle. Sources as diverse as the *Bloomberg Report* and the American Association of Retired Persons suggest that baby boomers make up the greatest proportion of guests at the taboo-breaking table. Named for the jump in birth rates after World War II, boomers range in age from their early fifties to late sixties, and as they still control much of the wealth and power in the US, remain a force to be reckoned with. Hardly the heedless youths suspected of overrunning the death movement, boomers are survivors of war, of illness and of increasingly fraught health-care systems. They've watched their parents die, and some have had the misfortune of losing children too. And yet, as Shannon Pettypiece puts it for *Bloomberg*, 'For the generation that brought on the sexual revolution, led the anti-war movement and turned their midlife crises into a time for reinvention and self-improvement, baby boomers are trying now to have it their way right to the very end.' But of course, death is one thing we cannot fully control – and this makes up a great deal of the conversation. If something happens unexpectedly, what would my wishes be? Do I want to be on life support? Do I want an open casket? Are my affairs in order? In other words, the champions of the 'good death' today are people who are frequently still healthy. We're alive, and this is the time, say the diners and cafe-goers, to do something about death.

Most of the articles, books, essays and commentary about the death-at-dinner and death-positive movements agree on one salient point. They all consider this present age to be the most death-denying of any to precede it. The truth, of course, is more complicated. Taken as a whole, the human race has not suddenly begun to deny death – our brief survey of non-Western traditions stands as evidence. Death denial is a privilege, and, ironically, it's the privilege of the young, healthy and wealthy, and has come about largely thanks to Western advances in medicine. In the modern, technological West, we deny death because we *can*.

Where, in all of this, is the religious perspective? Though, as I've explained, even believers often opt for funerals at funeral homes rather than at churches, most faiths focus at least in part upon the afterlife (as well as upon death itself). Death dinners aren't just for discussing the before-death plan; they're for re-engaging with what, if anything, comes after it. The cafes and dinners frequently begin with ice-breakers on topics you're generally warned to avoid: religion and politics, family tradition and personal belief. One point comes up in a variety of guises: is there life after death? This question hangs behind so many death rituals, and yet rarely are such things spoken of in public, especially among strangers. This is true of the US as well, even though – at least from the outside – it appears to be a nation steeped in (rather noisy) expression and discussion of religion.

As mentioned earlier, the US remains a secular state; its laws have been intentionally detached from the religious practices of its people. The point of that separation is to protect those who want to practise their faith, meaning Muslims, Jews, Hindus, Parsi, Buddhists and many, many others who call the US home are able to deal with life, birth and death according to their beliefs without legal infringement. In theory, that is. The reality is always much, much more complicated. Keeping the law from influencing or being influenced by religion can be a tricky business, and some things simply aren't allowed. The Parsis (a Zoroastrian group in India/South Asia) would prefer a kind of sky burial, like Tibetans – and in Mumbai, they used an area called the Tower of Silence to lay out their dead to the elements. But neither this practice, nor sky burial, is permitted in the US, for a variety of health and safety reasons.

Other means of faith practice run aground on prejudice; the terrorist attacks of 9/11 have resulted in suspicion and discrimination against Muslims practising their faith in the US, as well as other Western countries. And, perhaps more surprising to those unfamiliar with the US, even the 70 per cent of Americans who identify as Christians divide themselves among multiple denominations; one may be distinctly unwelcome in the home territory of another. Given so much divergence and difference, not only between 'believers' and 'unbelievers' but also among diverse faith groups, who would feel perfectly at ease discussing the afterlife, even with a friend? Yet for most of the world and for most of history, humans *have* believed in an afterlife, and many millions still do. Even so, believing in something beyond death does not necessarily make death easier to process – why should it? We mourn because we have lost; the cut is deep, the amputation complete. I once overheard the following accusation in a conversation between friends: 'Well, but you believe in heaven – and that's cheating', as if belief alone removes all sense of pain. The Torajans may believe the dead are still with us; the Day of the Dead festival may celebrate the permeable boundary between life and death; the Tibetans may see death as a rebirth – but the grief of those who mourn is just as real for them as for the most secular in the West. And, as we learned from the Cambodians and even from the headhunters, belief without ritual (or belief when ritual is prohibited) only serves to deepen the searing sense of helplessness.

The organiser of the Toronto Death Cafe lights candles at the beginning of the meeting, saying: 'We light our past candle to honour those who came before us; our present candle for all of us here; and our future candles for those who we have not yet met.' There is nothing dogmatic about the gesture, but it opens up the room to a wider space – when it comes to death, we must be inclusive. No one should shut down one set of rituals because it does not happen to agree with another. Meaning-seeking, the search for answers, the need not only to memorialise but to have a place to put our memories and emotions, this is what makes us human. In her article for *The Star*, Katelyn Verstraten quotes a man who lost his daughter in a tragic car accident: 'Just about everything I do in my world, in my life today, is a reflection of that,' he said, 'I'm not going to spend my life doing anything that isn't rewarding and meaning-ful to me.' Death dinners and death cafes may appear, at first glance, to be fads, springing up in light of tragedy (the first of Underwood's cafes occurred in September 2011, with many following). But if this particular death movement proves fleet-ing, it will be replaced by something similar – because we, the living, have need of it.

What we call Western culture – and, indeed, other cul-tures in the developed and developing world – may have travelled far from the cyclical roots of birth and death that once made dying an expected and meaningful part of life.

Some rituals have been eschewed over time as passé, as part of a religious past to be left behind. Rather like the early Reformation believers, those who continue to practise their faiths do so within the wider structure of a secularised society and – especially in the US, where many of the Protestant sects mistrust certain symbolic practices – shy away from once pro-lific rituals. But let's set all that aside for a moment and look, truly look, through the lenses these chapters have provided. Like the Torajans and the Merina, I have been seeking out the relationship between feasting and dying. Like the headhunt-ing tribesmen, we all have rage that needs a home. Like the Victorians, we all strive to make and keep memorials that reflect just how much the dead are still with us – and like the Wari, each of us may carry the dead away with us, in our very skin. In the West, our ancestors struggled to throw off the yoke of religious dogma; a version of that same struggle later took place with advances in medicine and technology, and the fight for patient autonomy. We look far and away, as through a distant and darkening mirror, only to find ourselves again. The rituals we have left behind follow us, reappearing in new ways, and that should be met with its own celebration. Why haven't we developed truly 'new' practices to replace old ones? Possibly because nothing is ever really 'new'. The rituals of early man cast long shadows. The contours have changed, enlarged and expanded over thousands of years, and each generation leaves its imprint. Whether we count ourselves as believers or non-believers, we should not fear choosing from the practices of the past for our ongoing traditions. The point is that we should be able to choose: to think about what we want, what we need, to discuss our choice with others and to let it help us when the time comes

What is a good ritual? Something that works to help and heal. I know of a Russian Orthodox priest who uses the teachings of Buddha when counselling soldiers struggling with trauma. The abused women's shelter mentioned in Chapter One incorporated Native American rites of passage – and there are many other examples where aspects of once-religious traditions have been incorporated for non-religious purposes. That sort of recombination isn't failure. It's an example of the evolving practices of our changing contexts. Like new shoots after a hard winter, poking through the snow with brilliant, longed-for green, these practices can lift the senses, slake thirst, provide new paths in a world wholly different from the one that existed before Death came to dinner. The most difficult aspect of all, however, is still the timing.

We cannot wait until death happens to talk about death. It's a bit like waiting until winter to gather in the grain. Why not meet now, talk now, while the sun is still warm on your back? That's the value of death's summer coat.

Epilogue

BEGINNING
AT THE END

In August of 2014, I stood to the left of a hammered-copper basin in a partially finished foyer that still smelled of drying plaster and new paint. I stood in a circle with two dozen others. Behind me, tall beeswax tapers flickered, standing upright in fine sand; in front of me, a young boy carried a pot of incense round and round the basin. Prayers were chanted aloud, and, as I didn't understand most of them, they seemed to me the humming cadence of summer cicadas. The warmth, the glow, the incense and the chanting infused the small space, and though I could still see the unpacked boxes (and though a workman periodically appeared outside the tall windows), the moment had a kind of magic in it. Something communal and sacred surrounded us, but this was not a funeral. The celebration here concerned new life: the Orthodox baptism of my infant nephew, my brother's third son.

I want to conclude by taking a closer look at beginnings. In Chapter One, I said that most of us have difficulty maintaining two ideas at once, and so it's hard for us to recognise something as both an event *and* a process. It's hard for us to put things together if they have divergent characters, and it's even harder to hold two opposing ideas in our minds at once. How can science exist alongside belief, or medicine be performed alongside spiritual or cultural ritual? Our examination of different cultures shows that it *is* possible . . . but we need not look so far away. At the furthest reaches of memory, in our first imaginings, many of us had just such impossible ideas. As I stood in the hall of my brother's Orthodox Church, I found myself remembering my grandfather's funeral. The newly dead need our care and attention; their passing away needs to be marked by some tangible ritual. Now, I stood at the baptismal font and thought the same about the newly born. Regardless of which system of belief we ascribe to, life's events require memorialising. And I wondered: is this something each generation needs to learn? Or is it something we collectively knew once, but have since forgotten?

I've had a rambling sort of life. My first memories are of Arizona (and a horse's nose; I was fond of feeding it rocks). My first memories of *home*, as I understand it, are of my grandmother's house – the one with the bluebells and stray cats. I lived with my grandparents and mother for my first four years, and I considered my grandfather also a father, as my parents divorced when I was just a few months old. My mother remarried, my brother came along and I was adopted into a new family structure by the time I was old enough for school, but my grandparents remained 'parents', too, in my young estimation. When I lost them many years later, I lost 'parents'; someday, when I lose my mother and father, I will be twice an orphan – three times if you count my biological father, who died when I was a toddler. I've had four last names. I have two half-brothers, one of whom I've met only once; the other, with whom I was raised, I consider soul of my soul. I had to juggle a great deal in my young head about who I was and where I was 'really' from – but I had surprisingly little trouble. Though my family had no organised religion, we were grounded in being just and kind, in working hard and in doing for yourself. In the absence of either prohibition or inclination towards established beliefs, I grew up believing that almost anything was possible. God and magic could both be real, along with elves and unicorns, witches and ghosts. And I lived in a place that supported rather than restricted that kind of thinking.

My brother and I grew up in an underground house in the Peabody Coal lands of southern Ohio. The mines have been abandoned, but great swathes of stripped ground remain, covered in pine and tall grass (about the only things that will grow in such depleted soil). Forested areas don't show the same scars, but may be riddled with sinkholes; both surface and underground mining took place in Coshocton County, beginning in the 1830s. Our home and the fifty acres surrounding it nestled between enormous tracts of Peabody Coal land now used for public hunting. It seemed to me a great and never-ending wilderness, with the exciting possibility of hidden mineshafts. We played elaborate games, made up stories, told tales. My brother and I had our own rich world, created with the glee of youth and without much oversight from adults or, as we lived far from town, other children.

That doesn't mean all was sweetness and light. We decided witches lived in the woods to the west, and that a demon might haunt the woods to the south. Most children believe in monsters. I may have been slightly unusual in that I wrote all of ours down, crafting them into stories that we rehearsed and revised. As we came across new things – new ideas, new monsters – we incorporated them. Children can be remarkably teleological; our system was fluid but sensibly interested in cause and effect. Dead trees lined the western wood: of course they did, because the witches lived there. One of the trees fell over and crushed a thorn bush. Naturally, the witches were trying to get out, or hoping we would go in. No one told us otherwise. So why not?

There may have been trauma in my childhood, but there was also enormous freedom. As I've listened in on the games of other children – my nieces and nephews, and the children of friends – I've noticed the same open, broad thinking. I suspect that most children, given the opportunity to play, will construct equally malleable and magical worlds. Why don't we make new rituals? We did; we have; we do. The trick is to retain their essence later, when we no longer see the world lit up with magic and possibility.

We all believe in something, and beliefs shift and change as we do. The assumption is sometimes made that religious people 'believe' and atheists 'do not', but that's far too black and white. Someone who believes in God or in gods may not accept all tenets of that belief, or hold to parts of it through tradition or memory rather than devout faith. Meanwhile, I have friends who profess no official religion but who nonetheless believe in something larger than the self – in humanity, in unselfishness, even in fate. Finding our way towards better rituals to mourn our dead and express our grief need not be markedly different from other way-finding. I've suggested that death has been sanitised and rendered unfamiliar in many Western cultures, and I'm not alone. Then again, there are cultures *within* cultures. It's humanity's misfortune that we greet difference with so much suspicion; how much better it would be if we opened up to the possibility of other ways of doing things. This openness begins with conversation – it begins with story – it begins with the death cafes and death salons, and perhaps it finds its clearest expression in the rising popularity of the grief memoir.

Until 2005, when Joan Didion published *The Year of Magical Thinking*, writings on grief were relatively hard to find – though they did exist. In *A Grief Observed,* published in 1961, C. S. Lewis called his writing after the death of his wife 'a defence against total collapse, a safety-valve'. A few years later, Elisabeth Kübler-Ross made much the same point with her five stages of grief; it's necessary to share the story, she said, in whatever form. It's one way to take the single devastating, dead-end event and turn it back into a process. We may not, like our ancestors, think of dying as something that happens to the soul after the physical death – that view of death really and truly was a process, with its own hurdles to overcome in the underworld. Instead, grief becomes the process, and a process needs stages, signposts and landmarks to help us see where we've been and where we are going.

The written word will always be mediated, and so perhaps it can never fully express or reproduce the raw pain of loss; but what it can do is introduce personal, individual loss into a narrative that others can share and relate to and take comfort in, a communal event. We could even argue that Facebook memorials and other digital media do the same: that they allow us to recontextualise our individual loss, and all of its confusion and frustration, into something that can be communicated. Joyce Carol Oates has remarked on her own 'accidental' memoir of loss, *A Widow's Story*, that 'the act of writing is an act of attempted comprehension, and, in a childlike way, control; we are so baffled and exhausted by what has happened, we want to imagine that giving words to the unspeakable will make it somehow our own.' But it's also true that by telling it, we make the story someone else's, and so the load of grief becomes shareable and, in a sense, more bearable.

We are narrative creatures, compelled to make sense of our surroundings through stories, and the stories we tell matter. The stories my brother and I told each other as children mattered; the stories his children and their children will tell also matter. Perhaps most important of all, the stories we tell *ourselves* matter. In writing this book, I've found myself looking with fresh eyes at aspects of death and dying I'd forgotten, or not previously considered. I've also found myself speaking to my family members and my spouse about mortality with increased freedom (and urgency). What kind of rituals will be meaningful to me or to those who remain after I die? I am attracted to green burial, and I hope to be buried with as little environmental impact as possible, but as I've spoken to loved ones, I've realised that I'm more interested in knowing what will matter most to them. Taking a cue from the death dinners, I've arranged a 'death date' with my husband, a time for us to speak candidly about our feelings. Are there things we would incorporate from the dying practices of my family? Or others we'd like to add from other cultural practices we've grown familiar with, and respect?

This process of listening and learning from each other goes on all around us – was going on, for instance, at my nephew's baptism. My brother and his family are converts to Christian orthodoxy (the Orthodox Church of America). The rituals practised there are almost as new to them as they are to me, but they have made them part of their experience, their world. I watched the priest bless the water, dropping oil into the font where it blossomed under the lights, and, though not a member myself, I felt connected to those gathered there. That sense of connection through participation is also reflected in the work of Paul Koudounaris, who feels a special connection to the practices in Bolivia he has witnessed and the decorated skeletons he photographs. These chapters have been about 'putting on' rituals, but they have also been about telling tales new to us – or rather, reinventing and reinvigorating old tales, learning from them and from each other. In our approach to death, as in our approach to living, I believe in better stories – and plenty of revision.

NOTES

~⌒

Page 17, It is one of the oldest surviving medical texts...
Michael Worton and Nana Wilson-Tagoe, *National Healths: Gender, Sexuality and Health in a Cross-Cultural Context* (London: Routledge Cavendish, 2004).

Page 18, If a child died before marrying...
Michael Kerrigan, *The History of Death* (London: Amber Books, 2007), 12.

Page 19, In February 2009, a team led by psychologist Alfonso Caramazza...
Nicole Branan, 'Are Our Brains Wired for Categorization? Our Innate Brain Structure Reflects How We Classify the World Around Us', *Scientific American*, 8 January 2009.

Page 21, Sociologist Allan Kellehear...
Based upon the work of Marais. Allan Kellehear, *A Social History of Dying* (Cambridge: Cambridge University Press, 2007), 13.

Page 22, 'dying' says Kellehear...
Ibid., 13.

Page 23, 'Here the "philosophical" point ends,'...
Ibid., 15.

Page 26, Some argue intentional burials happened...
Francesco d'Errico et al., 'Archaeological Evidence for the Emergence of Language, Symbolism, and Music – An Alternative Multidisciplinary Perspective', *Journal of World Prehistory* 17.1 (March 2003), 25.

Page 27, Among the Arunta, Frazer describes...
Sir James Frazer, *The Belief in Immortality and the Worship of the Dead: Volume 1* (1913), 373.

Page 29, It involved memory retrieval...
Harald Gündel et al., 'Functional Neuroanatomy of Grief: An FMRI Study', *American Journal of Psychiatry* (2003).

Page 30, Those who survived had witnessed horrific deaths...
Devon E. Hinton et al., 'Normal Grief and Complicated Bereavement Among Traumatized Cambodian Refugees: Cultural Context and the Central Role of Dreams of the Dead', *Culture, Medicine, and Psychiatry* 37(3) (2013), 427–64.

Page 31, Cambodians believe that dreams are powerful...
Ibid., 435.

Page 31, The ceremony gives blessing...
Ibid., Table 2.

Page 33, The anxiety of the early twentieth century...
Allan V. Horwitz and Jerome C. Wakefield, *The Loss of Sadness: How Psychiatry Transformed Normal Sorrow into Depressive Disorder* (Oxford: Oxford University Press, 2007), 3.

Page 33, In the US, the diagnosis and treatment of depression...
Ibid., 4.

Page 33, In Germany, rates rose by 70 per cent...
'Germany's New "Great Depression"', BBC News, 18 April 2005. <http://news.bbc.co.uk/1/hi/world/europe/4456087.stm> (last accessed 26 October 2014).

Page 35, For bereavement, the DSM defines...
Horwitz and Wakefield, *The Loss of Sadness*, 9.

Page 39, 'Death is not necessary . . .'
Adam Leith Gollner, *The Book of Immortality: The Science, Belief, and Magic Behind Living Forever* (New York: Scribner, 2013).

Page 39, In 2009, Kurzweil (the 'thinking machine')...
Amy Willis, 'Immortality only 20 years away says scientist', *The Telegraph*, 22 September 2009, <http://www.telegraph.co.uk/science/science-news/6217676/Immortality-only-20-years-away-says-scientist.html> (last accessed 26 October 2014).

Page 39, American molecular geneticist Bill Andrews...
Linda Carroll, 'Scientists say they're close to unlocking the secrets of immortality', *Today*, 13 December 2011, <http://www.today.com/id/45654223/ns/today-today_health/t/scientists-say-theyre-close-unlocking-secrets-immortality/#.VE1oFMmBBws> (last accessed 26 October 2014).

Page 40, In an article critiquing the 'survivor narrative'...
Mark A. Lewis, 'From Victim to Victor: *Breaking Bad* and the Dark Potential of the Terminally Empowered', *Culture, Medicine, and Psychiatry* 37(4) (2013).

Page 40, Contemporary western culture is built on denial...
Kellehear, *A Social History of Dying*, 55.

Page 41, In March 2012, *Culture, Medicine, and Psychiatry* published the work of Wozniak and Allen...
D. F. Wozniak and K. N. Allen, 'Ritual and Performance in Domestic Violence Healing: From Survivor to Thriver Through Rites of Passage', *Culture, Medicine, and Psychiatry* 36(1) (2012), 80–101.

Page 46, Reflection on death among Buddhists…
Michael D. Coogan, *Illustrated Guide to World Religions* (Oxford: Oxford University Press, 2003), 192.

Page 46, As Michael Coogan, professor emeritus of religious studies…
Ibid., 192.

Page 47, Buddhist meditation master…
Chögyam Trungpa Rinpoche, 'Commentary', *Tibetan Book of the Dead* (London: Shambhala, 2000), 1.

Page 48, Now when the bardo of the moment…
The Tibetan Book of the Dead, trans. Francesca Fremantle and Chögyam Trungpa (London: Shambhala, 2000), 98.

Page 50, 'Nearly every book on bereavement enraged me,'
Virginia Ironside, 'Nearly every book I read on bereavement enraged me', *The Independent*, 19 April 1996, <http://www.independent.co.uk/life-style/nearly-every-book-i-read-on-bereavement-enraged-me-1305591.html> (last accessed 26 October 2014).

Page 51, a grief that lasts too long is…
'Sometimes Grief Becomes Complicated, Unresolved or Stuck', 4Therapy.com, <http://www.4therapy.com/life-topics/grief-loss/sometimes-grief-becomes-complicated-unresolved-or-stuck-2249> (last accessed 26 October 2014).

Page 52, When Rosaldo asked the tribesmen…
Renato Rosaldo, 'Grief and a Headhunter's Rage', in Antonius C. G. M. Robben, ed., *Death, Mourning, and Burial: A Cross-Cultural Reader* (Oxford: Blackwell, 2004), 168.

Page 53, The Ilongot corrected him…
Ibid., 169.

Page 54, the 'anger at abandonment is irreducible…'
Ibid., 175.

Page 56, Anthropologist Beth Conklin describes…
Beth A. Conklin, '"Thus are Our Bodies, Thus was Our Custom": Mortuary Cannibalism in Amazonian Society', *American Ethnologist* 22:1 (February 1995), 75–101.

Page 57, Richard Sugg, author of *Mummies, Cannibals, Vampires*…
Richard Sugg, *Mummies, Cannibals, Vampires: The History of Corpse Medicine from the Renaissance to the Victorians* (London: Routledge, 2011), 15.

Page 57, Powdered skull made frequent appearances…
Mary Roach, *Stiff: The Curious Lives of Human Cadavers* (New York: W. W. Norton & Company, 2003), 233.

Page 58, One of the more infamous cases…
Ibid, 17.

Page 59, The vampire, says Paul Barber…
Paul Barber, *Vampires, Burial and Death* (New Haven: Yale University Press, 1988).

Page 61, 'dead people became a very significant part…'
'New study looks at why ancient South American culture mummified its dead.'
PRI's The World, 14 August 2012, <http://www.pri.org/stories/2012-08-14/
new-study-looks-why-ancient-south-american-culture-mummified-its-dead>
(last accessed 26 October 2014).

Page 61, 'the faces have been repainted several times'
Joann Fletcher, 'Mummies Around the World', *BBC History*, 17 February 2011,
<http://www.bbc.co.uk/history/ancient/egyptians/mummies_01.shtml>
(last accessed 26 October 2014).

Page 62, 'that our relationships with other humans…'
Kelli Swazey, 'Life that doesn't end with death,' transcript, *TEDMED* 13:54,
April 2013.

Page 62, Anthropologist Jane C. Wellenkamp refers…
Jane C. Wellenkamp, 'Notions of Grief and Catharsis Among the Toraja', *American
Ethnologist* 15.3 (August 1988), 486–500.

Page 63, David Graeber of the University of Chicago…
David Graeber, 'Dancing with Corpses Reconsidered: An Interpretation of
famadihana (in Arivonimamo, Madagascar)', *American Ethnologist* 22.2 (May 1995),
258–78.

Page 64, According to Ken Jeremiah…
Ken Jeremiah, 'Buried Alive: The Forgotten Practice of Self-Mummification',
Virginia Review of Asian Studies (2010).

Page 66, In referring to *All Souls Day*…
Stanley Brandes, *Skulls to the Living, Bread to the Dead* (Oxford: Blackwell, 2007),
29.

Page 66, a will from 1344 asked that heirs…
Ibid., 29.

Page 66, offerings might include 'tamales, oranges, sugarcane…'
Jesús Angel Ochoa Zazueta, *La muerte y los muertos : culto, servicio, ofrenda y humor de
una comunidad* (Mexico: Secretaría de Educación Pública, 1974). Cited by Brandes.

Page 66, Brandes asks if this process is itself a denial of death…
Stanley Brandes, 'Sugar, Colonialism, and Death: On the Origins of Mexico's Day
of the Dead', *Comparative Studies in Society and History* 39.2 (April 1997), 270–99.

Page 71, 'For us,' he explains, 'death is an impassable...'
Interview: Paul Koudounaris, 30 March 2014. [Interview with the author]

Page 72, Philippe Ariès, author of *The Hour of Death*, calls this 'tame' death.
Philippe Ariès, *The Hour of Our Death*, trans. Helen Weaver (New York: Oxford
University Press, 1981).

Page 73, 'If you can have a quiet death...'
Susan Spencer, 'Experiencing a Good Death', *Sunday Morning*, CBS News,
27 April 2014, <http://www.cbsnews.com/news/experiencing-a-good-death/>
(last accessed 26 October 2014).

Page 74, 'There's always something physiologically that we can tweak...'
Ibid.

Page 75, It destroyed lives throughout Europe...
John Kelly, *The Great Mortality* (New York: Harper Collins, 2005), xii.

Page 77, Something more was necessary...
Ibid., 15.

Page 79, 'as our city sunk into this affliction and misery...'
Giovanni Boccaccio, *The Decameron*: 'Boccaccio on the Plague',
trans. David Burr, <http://www.history.vt.edu/Burr/Boccaccio.html>
(last accessed 26 October 2014).

Page 79, the 'Great Mortality', a time of 'unremitting death'...
Kelly, *The Great Mortality*, 294.

Page 81, 'No one wanted rotting bodies hauled through their front yards...'
Allison Meier, 'Bring Out Your Dead to These Corpse Roads', *Atlas Obscura*,
10 June 2014, <http://www.atlasobscura.com/articles/bring-out-your-dead-
to-these-corpse-roads> (last accessed 26 October 2014).

Page 81, many Europeans still hoped to be buried in 'hallowed ground'...
R. C. Finucane, 'Sacred Corpse, Profane Carrion: Social Ideas and Death in
the Later Middle Ages', in Joachim Whaley, ed., *Mirrors of Mortality* (New York:
St. Martin's Press, 1982), 42.

Page 82, those approaching death could see 'over the boundary'...
Ibid., 51.

Page 82, 'Inebriate conviviality...'
Ralph Houlbrooke, 'Death, Church, and Family in England Between the Late
Fifteenth and the Early Eighteenth Centuries', in Houlbrooke, ed., *Death, Ritual,
and Bereavement* (London: Routledge, 1989), 35.

Page 82, When Henry VII died in 1509...
Paul S. Fritz, 'From "Public" to "Private": The Royal Funerals in England 1500–1830', in Joachim Whaley, ed., *Mirrors of Mortality* (New York: St. Martin's Press, 1982).

Page 84, historian Peter Wilson marks its beginning with murder...
Peter Wilson, *The Thirty Years War: Europe's Tragedy* (Cambridge, MA: Belknap Press, 2011).

Page 84, The war officially came to an end in 1648...
'Treaty of Westphalia: Peace Treaty Between the Holy Roman Emperor and the King of France and Their Respective Allies', *Avalon Project*, Yale Law School, <http://avalon.law.yale.edu/17th_century/westphal.asp> (last accessed 26 October 2014).

Page 86, Turning skeletons into martyrs required labour.
Interview: Paul Koudounaris, 30 March 2014. [Interview with the author]

Page 87, However, the desire to venerate the dead...
Houlbrooke, 'Death, Church, and Family', 39.

Page 87, As the dawn of the eighteenth century approached...
Clare Gittings, *Death, Burial and the Individual in Early Modern England* (London: Routledge, 1984).

Page 87, Rev. Henry Newcombe claims in 1654...
Quoted in Houlbrooke, 'Death, Church, and Family', 39.

Page 87, The imagery and the symbol retain importance...
Houlbrooke, 'Death, Church, and Family', 41.

Page 88, 'With swollen legs...'
Leslie Clarkson, *Death, Disease and Famine in Pre-Industrial England* (Dublin: Gill & Macmillan, 1975), 151.

Page 89, Locke questioned the basis for kingly authority...
John McCrystal, 'Revolting Women', *History of Political Thought* 14:2 (1993), 189–203; see p. 191.

Page 89, He viewed certain revolutions...
Ibid., 195.

Page 90, 'remained in the shadows, secondary, almost irrelevant'
Roy Porter, 'Death and the Doctors in Georgian England', in Ralph Houlbrooke, ed., *Death, Ritual, and Bereavement* (London: Routledge, 1989), 81.

Page 90, 'If I had a pen in my hand now...'
Ibid., 85.

Page 90, ... medicine became primarily interested in prolonging life.
Ibid, 85.

Page 91, More importantly, death began to be perceived as an untimely event...
Stella Malley O'Gordon, 'Death and Dying in Contemporary Society', *Journal of Advanced Nursing* 27 (1998), 1127–35; see p. 1129.

Page 91, only 200 of every 1,000 babies born in France...
John McManners, *Death and the Enlightenment* (Oxford: Oxford University Press, 1981), 5.

Page 92, Roy Porter acknowledges the influence of doctors in changing the 'face of death'...
Porter, 'Death and the Doctors in Georgian England', 79.

Page 94, Prayers would be said...
McManners, *Death and the Enlightenment*, 270.

Page 94, The Catholic clergy were actively discouraged...
Ibid., 271.

Page 94, both the pious and the Enlightenment rationalists of the eighteenth century...
Ibid., 299.

Page 95, In Germany, thanks in part to the Thirty Years' War...
Ibid., 82.

Page 95, the *Sorgemann* was the chief mourner...
Ibid., 89.

Page 96, The main mourners followed the corpse...
Ibid., 95.

Page 96, One hundred and twenty-one people...
Ibid., 95.

Page 96, The monument of Marshall Saxe...
David Irwin, 'Sentiment and Antiquity: European Tombs 1750–1830', in Joachim Whaley, ed., *Mirrors of Mortality* (New York: St. Martin's Press, 1982), 131.

Page 96, France's military power is further secured...
Ibid., 133.

Page 97, McManners points to an eighteenth-century lawyer
McManners, *Death and the Enlightenment*, 63.

Page 97, Author Mike Rendell has recorded the funeral arrangements for the wife of his British ancestor, Richard Hall.
Mike Rendell, 'A Funeral 233 Years Ago – 18th Century Style – And the Undertakers Bill!' *Georgian Gentleman: the Musings of Richard Hall 1729–1801.* Weblog. <http://mikerendell.com/death-in-the-afternnon-18th-century-style-and-the-undertakers-bill/>

Page 104, 'When the corpse was brought out...'
John Evelyn, quoted in Michael Kerrigan, *The History of Death* (London: Amber Books, 2007), 143.

Page 105, St Martin-in-the-Fields, which was only about 200 feet square...
Ibid., 143.

Page 106, Britain's first major public cemeteries...
Ibid., 148.

Page 106, Kensal Green, Norwood, Highgate...
Ibid., 149.

Page 107, stripping a taboo subject of 'offensive' overtones.
Eliecer Fernandez, 'The Language of Death', *SKY Journal of Linguistics* 19 (2006), 101–30.

Page 107, The word 'obituary' is itself a euphemism...
Ibid.

Page 108, The more we understand ourselves...
Sarah Tarlow, 'The Aesthetic Corpse in Nineteenth-Century Britain', *Thinking Through the Body* (New York: Kluwer, 2002), 86.

Page 108, 'from the eighteenth century we see increasing efforts...'
Ibid., 91.

Page 109, 'Relics work as traces of a life and body completed and disappeared...'
Deborah Lutz, 'The Dead Still Among Us: Victorian Secular Relics, Hair Jewelry, and Death Culture', *Victorian Literature and Culture* 39 (2011), 127–42, p. 128.

Page 110, In the first year of mourning a widow wore...
Kerrigan, *The History of Death*, 155.

Page 111, Deborah Lutz ... calls these 'secular relics'.
Lutz, 'The Dead Still Among Us'.

Page 111, the most common relics are associated with...
Barbara Drake Boehm, 'Relics and Reliquaries in Medieval Christianity', Metropolitan Museum of Art, <http://www.metmuseum.org/toah/hd/relc/hd_relc.htm> (last accessed 26 October 2014).

Page 111, Lutz describes the two sides of this trend...
Lutz, 'The Dead Still Among Us'.

Page 113, Relics like these became a virtual 'craze'...
Ibid.

Page 113, One from *Godey's Magazine* provides a range of choices...
Godey's Magazine 72–73 (1866).

Page 113, The *Illustrated London News* carried specialised advertisements...
Illustrated London News 53 (1868).

Page 113, 'the focus of mourning is no longer the mourned and their fame...'
Christiane Holm, 'Sentimental Cuts: Eighteenth-Century Mourning Jewelry with Hair', *Eighteenth-Century Studies* 39 (2004), 139–43.

Page 113, 'in the mourning dress, the outward sign of sorrow...'
Basil Montagu, quoted in Patricia Jalland, *Death in the Victorian Family* (Oxford: Oxford University Press, 1996), 302.

Page 114, Victorian etiquette manuals told their readers...
Ibid., 302.

Page 114, 'The dress for mid-summer or mid-winter is...'
Good Housekeeping, Hearst Corporation, 9 (1889), 113.

Page 115, 'crape flowers', though popular on the continent...
Millinery Trade Review, Marriotte and Co., 1 (1876), 51.

Page 115, full mourning is 'a hot and expensive dress'...
J. T. Buckingham, *The Polyanthos* 4 (1813), 189.

Page 116, 'What I always found most compelling...'
Steve DeGenero, 23 August 2013. [Interview with the author].

Page 118, DeGenero explains the daguerreotype as superior...
Steve DeGenero, 23 August 2013. [Interview with the author]

Page 119, 'Thinking about how the family and the photographer had to improvise...'
Ibid.

Page 121, 'Secure the Shadow...'
Jay Ruby, *Secure the Shadow: Death and Photography in America* (Cambridge: MIT Press, 1995).

Page 122, This new sort of mourning ephemera...
Jen Cadwallader, 'Spirit Photography and the Victorian Culture of Mourning', *Modern Language Studies* 37.2 (2008), 8–31, p. 14.

Page 125, People rarely kept bodies in their home...
Lutz, 'The Dead still Among Us'.

Page 128, To quote the title of a 2004 debate forum...
G. D. Guttmann, R. L. Drake and R. B. Trelease, 'To What Extent is Cadaver Dissection Necessary to Learn Medical Gross Anatomy? A Debate Forum', *The Anatomical Record* 281(1) (2004), 2–3.

Page 129, The news broke on 3 November 1832…
Lisa Rosner, 'The Horrid and True Story of Burke and Hare',
<http://burkeandhare.com/bhhome.html> (last accessed 27 October 2014).

Page 129, The investigation and trial…
Ibid.

Page 129, These new research methods…
Richardson, Ruth, *Death, Dissection and the Destitute* (University of Chicago Press, 2000).

Page 130, most of whom would never touch the body at all.
E. Ashworth Underwood, 'The "Fabrica" Of Andreas Vesalius: A Quatercentenary Tribute', *British Medical Journal* 1:4303 (26 June 1943), 795–6, p. 795.

Page 131, the presiding professors failed to comment on certain discrepancies…
Michael Mosely, *The Story of Science*: 'What is the Secret of Life?' BBC television, 25 May 2010.

Page 132, on at least one occasion, the specimen was still hanging from the gibbet…
Ibid.

Page 132, In Venice, Vesalius met artist Jan Stephan van Calcar,
Underwood, 'The "Fabrica" Of Andreas Vesalius', 795.

Page 132, 'in an age when the dead hand of medievalism…'
Ibid, 796.

Page 132, As a New York Public Library exhibit put it…
Sophia Vackimes, 'Seeing Is Believing: 700 Years of Scientific and Medical Illustration: A Review', *American Anthropologist*, New Series, 103:3 (September 2001), 809–12.

Page 132, 'What were Andreas Vesalius or Hieronymus Brunschwig…'
Ibid., 810.

Page 134, The 1832 Anatomy Act intended to provide greater access…
Richardson, *Death, Dissection and the Destitute*.

Page 134, 'If they were poor they imprisoned them…'
The Spectator, Vol 11, Published by FC. Westley, 1838. p. 531.

Page 134, In a Smithsonian article…
Bess Lovejoy, 'The Gory New York City Riot that Shaped American Medicine', *Smithsonian Magazine*, 17 June 2014.

Page 135, 'young gentlemen in this city who call themselves students of the physic…'
Ibid.

Page 135, in Boston in the 1840s, the influx of 'Irish paupers' shifted the balance...
John Harley Warner, 'Witnessing Dissection', in John Harley Warner and James Edmonson, eds., *Dissection: Photographs of a Rite of Passage in American Medicine 1880–1930* (New York: Blast Books, 2009).

Page 135, sentiments 'boiled over' in New York...
Lovejoy, 'The Gory New York City Riot', 2.

Page 135, Warner cites a similar example of public outcry...
Warner, 'Witnessing Dissection', 19.

Page 135, the 'prudent line of stealing only the bodies of the poor'
Ibid., 18.

Page 136, Anatomical specimens had become so necessary...
Michael Sappol, *A Traffic of Dead Bodies: Anatomy and Embodied Social Identity in Nineteenth-Century America* (Princeton: Princeton University Press, 2002).

Page 136, professional 'resurrectionists' held sway.
Warner, 'Witnessing Dissection', 17.

Page 136, the coffin would be uncovered...
Ibid., 17.

Page 136, The bodies were stripped of incriminating identification...
Ibid., 17.

Page 136, 'black bodies disinterred from southern graves'
Ibid., 17.

Page 136, Resurrectionists in urban areas worked late at night...
Knott, 'Popular Attitudes', 2.

Page 137, 'You are now upon that stage of life...'
Warner, 'Witnessing Dissection', 9.

Page 138, suggested that women were too 'Fickle' and had a 'Softness and Timorousness'...
François Fénelon, *Instructions for the Education of a Daughter* (London: Printed for Jonah Bowyer, 1709), 13, 184.

Page 138, dissection defiled a woman's 'moral constitution'
Warner, 'Witnessing Dissection', 9.

Page 138, declared the study of anatomy a 'hymn in honor of the creator'
Ibid., 10.

Page 139, Prior to the 1800s, Europe had 'superior access' to corpses...
Ibid., 9.

Page 139, Edmonson suggests that this iconography may have served as a kind of inspiration.
James Edmonson, 'Afterword: Curatorial Observations on the Dissection Image', in John Harley Warner and James Edmonson, eds, *Dissection: Photographs of a Rite of Passage in American Medicine 1880–1930* (New York: Blast Books, 2009), 193.

Page 140, by 1900, the development of Kodak's 'Brownie' camera...
Ibid., 195.

Page 140, The images occasionally bear inscriptions...
Warner, 'Witnessing Dissection', 13, 25.

Page 142, Some have names, like 'A Student's Dream'...
Warner and Edmonson, *Dissection*, 143.

Page 142, 'wilful transgressions of funeral custom'
Michael Sappol, *Dream Anatomy* (Washington, DC: National Library of Medicine, 2006), 11.

Page 143, this very familiarity 'contributed to a legacy of distrust'
Warner, 'Witnessing Dissection', 26.

Page 143, 'a new convention of silence'
Ibid., 27.

Page 145, there was an erotic power wielded by anatomists...
Ibid., 27.

Page 146, 'Detachment', Warner remarks, citing critics from the late 1970s...
Warner, 'Witnessing Dissection', 28.

Page 147, Most people in Switzerland died at home...
Laura Newman, 'Elisabeth Kübler-Ross, psychiatrist and pioneer of the death-and-dying movement', *British Medical Journal* 329: 7466 (11 September 2004), 627.

Page 148, Through the use of idealised, piecemeal, intensely coloured images...
Sappol, *Dream Anatomy*, 46.

Page 148, we pay for 'health and funerary professionals to place a veil between us and death...'
Ibid., 70.

Page 148, He is able to produce them through 'plastination'
Christine Quigley, *Dissection on Display: Cadavers, Anatomists and Public Spectacle* (Jefferson, NC: McFarland & Company, 2012).

Page 148, it's partly these 'posthumous personalities' that draws crowds
Ibid., 183.

Page 149, 'comprehensive, self-paced learning programme that explores anatomy from four different perspectives'
Sarah Griffiths, 'Not for the faint-hearted! Medical website lets you virtually dissect dead bodies', *Daily Mail*, 18 June 2014, <http://www.dailymail.co.uk/sciencetech/article-2660323/Not-faint-hearted-Medical-website-lets-virtually-dissect-dead-bodies.html> (last accessed 27 October 2014).

Page 149, SynDaver™ hopes to develop synthetic humans
'About', SynDaver™ Labs, <http://syndaver.com/about/> (last accessed 27 October 2014).

Page 152, 'One young woman's tribute describes...'
Roach, *Stiff*, 38.

Page 153, 'It's like the difference between watching somebody show you how to drive a car, and actually driving it.'
Kelly Grant, 'Dissection Debate: Why Are Medical Schools Cutting Back on Dissection?' *The Globe and Mail*, <http://www.theglobeandmail.com/life/health-and-fitness/health/dissection-debate-why-are-medical-schools-cutting-back-on-cadavers/article18296300/> (last accessed 27 October 2014).

Page 153, Plastinates or anatomical models, the authors argue, 'do not allow such a way of thinking'
Horst-Werner Korf et al., 'The Dissection Course – Necessary and Indispensable for Teaching Anatomy to Medical Students', *Annals of Anatomy* 190 (2008), 16–22.

Page 153, It is in the dissection laboratory, she explains...
Noelle Granger, 'Dissection Laboratory is Vital to Medical Gross Anatomy Education', *The Anatomical Record* 281B (2004), 6–8, p. 6.

Page 154, The 'first arduous step required of students in dissection courses is the cold objectivism of the cadaver'
Korf et al., 'The Dissection Course', 19.

Page 154, Kimberly Todd, in response to Granger's article, remarks that cadaver dissection is *not* universally necessary to all students...
Kimberly Todd, 'Prosection vs. Dissection, the Debate Continues: Rebuttal to Granger', *The Anatomical Record* 281B (2004), 12–14, p. 12.

Page 155, John Bertram, coordinator of anatomy teaching...
Grant, 'Dissection Debate'.

Page 155, In an anthropological study, Godeau found...
Emmanuelle Godeau, 'Dissecting Cadavers: Learning Anatomy or a Rite of Passage?' *Hektoen International: Medical Humanities* 1:5 (November 2009), <http://www.hektoeninternational.org/index.php?option=com_content&view=article&id=599> (last accessed 27 October 2014).

Page 155, Citing dissection as a 'privilege' denied to non-doctors...
Ibid.

Page 163, In 1969, feminist philosopher Simone de Beauvoir wrote, 'there is no such thing as a natural death...'
Simone De Beauvoir, *A Very Easy Death*, trans. Patrick O'Brian (London: André Deutsch/Weidenfeld & Nicolson, 1966).

Page 163, Los Angeles photographer Andrew George recently worked on a project entitled 'Right Before I Die'...
Andrew George, 'Right Before I Die,' <http://rightbeforeidie.com/rbid.html> (last accessed 27 October 2014).

Page 166, If the Hippocratic Oath requires a doctor to give assistance...
Louis Lasagna, 'Modern Hippocratic Oath', <http://guides.library.jhu.edu/content.php?pid=23699&sid=190964> (last accessed 27 October 2014).

Page 166, Medicine could not deal with the messy and disorderly process of death, and so 'quieted' patients with medicine...
B. McNamara, *Fragile Lives: Death, Dying, and Care* (Sydney: Allen and Unwin, 2001), 106.

Page 167, I have heard the arguments ... even in a thread on the *Daily Mail* website
'Do GPs Have Too Much Power?' *Mail Online*, 18 October 2011, <http://boards.dailymail.co.uk/health/10237941-do-gps-have-too-much-power.html> (last accessed 27 October 2014).

Page 167, shying away from mortality is an especially marked feature of American medical culture...
Peter Metcalf and Richard Huntington, *Celebrations of Death: An Anthropology of Mortuary Ritual* (Cambridge: Cambridge University Press, 1991).

Page 167, In their article 'Midwives Among the Machines', Raymond G. DeVries and Rebeca Barroso tell the story of a spontaneous birth...
Raymond G. DeVries and Rebeca Barroso, 'Midwives Among the Machines: Recreating Midwifery in the 20th Century', in Hilary Marland and Anne Marie Rafferty, eds, *Midwives, Society and Childbirth* (London: Routledge, 1997), 248, 249.

Page 169, 'If I'm lucky,' Bowron says, 'the family will recognise that their loved one's life is nearing its end...'
Craig Bowron, 'Our Unrealistic Views of Death, Through a Doctor's Eyes', *Washington Post*, 17 February 2012, <http://www.washingtonpost.com/opinions/our-unrealistic-views-of-death-through-a-doctors-eyes/2012/01/31/gIQAeaHpJR_story.html> (last accessed 27 October 2014).

Page 169, 'One powerful memory,' she writes, 'is from a patient named Stella...'
Bronnie Ware, 'I Regret the Way We Are Dying', *The Guardian*, 3 July 2014,
<http://www.theguardian.com/commentisfree/2014/jul/03/regret-dying-
palliative-care-nurse-top-5-regrets-prof-john-ashton> (last accessed 27 October
2014).

Page 170, 'All over the country people are spending their last days and weeks in
major discomfort...'
Ibid.

Page 170, By the Victorian era, and largely as a result of waning religious
influence and rising gentrification...
Kellehear, *A Social History of Dying*, 167.

Page 171, His achievement was followed in the 1950s by the invention and
widespread use of ventilators...
Michael DeGeorgia, 'History of Brain Death as Death: 1968 to the Present',
Journal of Critical Care 29 (2014), 673–8, p. 673.

Page 172, In 1954, Massachusetts neurologist Robert Schwab...
Ibid., 673.

Page 172, In 1959, however, fellow neurologists Mollaret and Goulon
disagreed...
P. Mollaret and M. Goulon, 'The Depassed Coma (Preliminary Memoir)', *Revue
neurologique* 101 (1959), 3–15.

Page 173, In 1968 an ad hoc committee gathered at Harvard to try and redefine
death in a new way.
DeGeorgia, 'History of Brain Death', 674.

Page 173, 'Any organ, brain or other, that no longer functions...'
Ibid., 675.

Page 173, For instance, because of the UK emphasis on brain*stem* rather than
EEG...
Ibid., 676.

Page 173, She remains on life support at a care facility in New Jersey...
Karina Ioffee and David DeBolt, 'Jahi McMath being kept at New Jersey hospital',
San Jose Mercury News, 18 June 2014, <http://www.mercurynews.com/
breaking-news/ci_25992852/jahi-mcmath-being-kept-alive-at-new-jersey>
(last accessed 27 October 2014).

Page 174, 'It never occurred to most of us...'
Cathy Shufro, 'A Doctor Learns to Cope with Death', *Yale Medicine* (Spring 2007),
41:3.

Page 175, Another physician, Dr Elaine Goodman, recently wrote…
Marshall Allen, 'What a New Doctor Learned About Medical Mistakes From Her Mom's Death', *ProPublica*, 9 January 2013.

Page 175, after Chen, as she tells it, 'turned away' from a patient she knew well…
Shufro, 'A Doctor Learns'.

Page 176, In America, a National Public Radio correspondent reported…
Joanne Silberner, 'Doctors and Death', *All Things Considered* (National Public Radio transcript), 4 January 1998, <http://www.npr.org/programs/death/980104. death.html> (last accessed 27 October 2014).

Page 178, In 2013, an article in the *Wall Street Journal* suggested residents were 'dangerously exhausted'…
'The Experts: Are Medical Residents Dangerously Exhausted?' *The Wall Street Journal*, 22 February 2013, <http://online.wsj.com/articles/SB1000142412788 7324503204578318763513170222> (last accessed 27 October 2014).

Page 179, many medical students in the UK are being asked to 'opt out' and work more hours…
Rebecca Smith, 'Junior doctors will be encouraged to opt out of Working Time Directive: Department of Health', *The Telegraph*, 22 July 2014, <http://www. telegraph.co.uk/health/healthnews/10980505/Junior-doctors-will-be-encouraged-to-opt-out-of-Working-Time-Directive-Department-of-Health. html> (last accessed 27 October 2014).

Page 180, 'concerns over the struggles and agonies of the spirit soon gave way…'
Kellehear, 180. (2007).

Page 183, 'Medicine is facing a crisis…'
David Bornstein, 'Medicine's Search for Meaning', *New York Times* Opinionator blog, 18 September 2013, <http://opinionator.blogs.nytimes.com/2013/09/ 18/medicines-search-for-meaning/?_php=true&_type=blogs&_r=0> (last accessed 27 October 2014).

Page 183, When Remen cried as the parents were informed of the death…
Ibid.

Page 184, 'Knowledge of the impending death may be uncertain…'
Kellehear, *A Social History of Dying*, 207.

Page 187, 'I believe death is considered taboo because it [the afterlife] is so unknown…'
Interview: Jane Carlyle, 29 July 2014. [Interview with the author; name changed to protect anonymity]

Page 195, Science might try to explain *why* we grieve…
Leeat Granek, 'Grief as Pathology: The Evolution of Grief Theory in Psychology
From Freud to the Present', *History of Psychology* 13:1 (2010), 46–73.

Page 195, …does nothing to support one's actual emotional state during
such times.
Gina Stepp, 'Give Sorrow More Than Words: The Neuroscience of
Grieving', *Vision*, <http://www.vision.org/visionmedia/grief-and-loss/
neuroscience/2166.aspx> (last accessed 27 October 2014).

Page 197, 'Our [plane] is still missing. How to move on?'
Jake Maxwell Watts and Celine Fernandez, 'Flight 17 Burial Delays Frustrate
Families', *The Wall Street Journal*, 19 July 2014, <Jake Maxwell Watts and
Celine Fernandez, 'Flight 17 Burial Delays Frustrate Families'> (last accessed
27 October 2014).

Page 197, 'without Andrew's body, I don't think we will ever get closure.
We can't move forward.'
Jacinta Carroll, '"We Can't Move Forward": Parents Plead to Be Allowed
to Bury Missing Boy', *Central Western Daily*, 21 June 2014, <http://www.
centralwesterndaily.com.au/story/2365804/we-cant-move-forward-parents-
plead-to-be-allowed-to-bury-missing-boy/> (last accessed 27 October 2014).

Page 198, he looks at regionalism, and describes eleven smaller 'nations'
Colin Woodard, *American Nations: A History of the Eleven Rival Regional Cultures of
North America* (New York: Viking, 2011).

Page 199, In a national study of American morticians, V. R. Pine discovered…
Metcalf and Huntington, *Celebrations of Death*, 194.

Page 199, 92 per cent of all deaths result in earth-burial.
Ibid., 194.

Page 201, The tightly organised funeral industry
Ibid., 199.

Page 201, 'in danger of losing the capacity to mark ritually the profound
significance of the experience of death'
Thomas G. Long, 'Why Jessica Mitford was Wrong', *Theology Today* (January
1999).

Page 201, 'this isn't a hospital and I don't provide a service – this is a business'
Cory Doctorow, 'Anonymous funeral director explains the big con behind
the industry, coffins, and embalming', *BoingBoing*, 11 August 2013, <http://
boingboing.net/2013/08/19/anonymous-funeral-director-exp.html> (last
accessed 27 October 2014).

Page 207, Callender describes as 'smoked glass, through which together we might glimpse death's outline'.
Rupert Callender et al. ed., *The Natural Death Handbook*, 5th edition (London: Strange Attractor, 2012).

Page 207, In Germany the dying can opt for woodland burial...
Marco Tosatti, 'Germany Sets Woodland Burial Trend', *The Vatican Insider*, 12 April 2012.

Page 208, The *San Francisco Gate* reported in 2013 that 'green burial' restores and preserves the land...
Rob Caughlan, '"Green burial" Restores, Preserves the Land', *SFGate*, 22 October 2013.

Page 208, the Foxfield Preserve of Ohio provides an alternative...
Foxfield Preserve, 'The Natural Burial Movement', <http://www.foxfieldpreserve.org/foxfield/the-natural-burial-movement/> (last accessed 27 October 2014).

Page 209, 'try to control what happens to your remains when you are no longer around to reap the joys or benefits of that control'
Roach, *Stiff*, 290.

Page 210, 'eternal reefs', places where concrete orbs of human remains help to expand or rebuild coral reef areas.
Stephanie Pappas, 'After Death: 8 Burial Alternatives That Are Going Mainstream', *Live Science*, 9 September 2011, <http://www.livescience.com/15980-death-8-burial-alternatives.html> (last accessed 27 October 2014).

Page 210, 'I am convinced that it is not the fear of death...'
Harold Kushner, *When All You've Ever Wanted Isn't Enough: The Search for a Life That Matters* (New York: Simon & Schuster, 2002).

Page 210, 'We don't get it right in this country...'
Bryony Gordon, 'Kirstie Allsopp: "I Don't Want the Next Generation of Women to Suffer the Same Heartache"', *The Telegraph*, 1 June 2014, <http://www.telegraph.co.uk/lifestyle/10868367/Kirstie-Allsopp-I-dont-want-the-next-generation-of-women-to-suffer-the-same-heartache.html)> (last accessed 27 October 2014).

Page 211, In June of 2014, one American family made headlines...
Alyssa Newcomb, 'Dead People Get Life-Like Poses at Their Funerals', ABC News, 13 June 2014, <http://abcnews.go.com/US/dead-people-life-poses-funerals/story?id=23456853> (last accessed 27 October 2014).

Page 212, 'when bereavement is no longer given public space in society or culture…'
Bradley Cornelius, 'Dr Candi Cann, Baylor University – The Mobility Of Modern Memorials', *Academic Minute*, WAMC Northeast Public Radio, 12 December 2013, <http://wamc.org/post/dr-candi-cann-baylor-university-mobility-modern-memorials> (last accessed 27 October 2014).

Page 213, 'What happens', Draeger asks, 'to the currency left in online accounts when passwords are not designated to the deceased's heirs?'
Dennis Draeger, 'Modern Memorials', *Innovations Solutions*, <http://www.innovationmanagement.se/2012/10/24/modern-memorials/> (last accessed 27 October 2014).

Page 213, 'I'm dogged by our messages [. . .] In some ways, it's worse that Facebook is almost all I have of her'
Julie Buntin, 'She's Still Dying on Facebook', *The Atlantic*, 6 July 2014, <http://www.theatlantic.com/technology/archive/2014/07/shes-still-dying-on-facebook/373904/> (last accessed 27 October 2014).

Page 215, 'will we begin to see a new emotion arise…'
Draeger, 'Modern Memorials'.

Page 217, 'intellectuals and independent thinkers engaged in the exploration of our shared mortality'
'About Us', Death Salon, <http://deathsalon.org/about-us/> (last accessed 27 October 2014).

Page 217, But these aims, lauded in an article called 'Death is Having a Moment' by Erika Hayasaki…
Erika Hayasaki, 'Death is Having a Moment', *The Altantic*, 25 October 2013. http://www.theatlantic.com/health/archive/2013/10/death-is-having-a-moment/280777/

Page 221, food has primarily been used in three different ways as it relates to death…
Sarah Troop, 'About Nourishing Death', <http://nourishingdeath.wordpress.com/about/> (last accessed 27 October 2014).

Page 221, Dr Christina Lee, author of *Feasting the Dead*, talks about how important funeral food was to early Anglo-Saxons…
Christina Lee, *Feasting the Dead: Food and Drink in Anglo-Saxon Burial Rituals* (Woodbridge, England and Rochester, NY: Boydell and Brewer, 2007).

Page 223, 'There's a *café philo*, which is a philosophical cafe…'
Deena Prichep, 'Death Cafes Breathe Life Into Conversations About Dying',
National Public Radio, 8 March 2013, <http://www.npr.org/2013/03/
08/173808940/death-cafes-breathe-life-into-conversations-about-dying> (last
accessed 27 October 2014).

Page 223, 'Talking about it can only be a good thing…'
Eleanor Tucker, 'What on Earth is a Death Cafe?', *The Guardian*, 21 March
2014, <http://www.theguardian.com/lifeandstyle/2014/mar/22/
death-cafe-talk-about-dying> (last accessed 27 October 2014).

Page 223, 'How have we got to the stage in our sanitised society…'
Ibid.

Page 224, Instead, she found herself 'directed upstairs to a bright, sunny room at
the cemetery's visitation centre'
Katelyn Verstraten, 'At a Death Café: A Life-affirming Experience', *The Star*,
1 August 2014, <http://www.thestar.com/news/insight/2014/07/20/at_a_
death_caf_a_lifeaffirming_experience.html> (last accessed 27 October 2014).

Page 225, 'For the generation that brought on the sexual revolution…'
Shannon Pettypiece, 'Death Dinners at Baby Boomers' Tables Take on Dying
Taboo', *The Bloomberg Report*, 24 September 2013, <http://www.bloomberg.
com/news/2013-09-24/death-dinners-at-baby-boomers-tables-take-on-
dying-taboo.html> (last accessed 27 October 2014).

Page 228, 'We light our past candle to honour those who came before us…'
Verstraten, 'At a Death Café'.

Page 236, writings on grief were relatively hard to find – though they did exist.
Raina Wallens, 'Does Sad Sell?', *The Rumpus*, 10 May 2011, <http://therumpus.
net/2011/05/does-sad-sell/> (last accessed 13 November 2014).

Page 236, 'a defence against total collapse, a safety-valve'
C. S. Lewis, *A Grief Observed* (London: Faber & Faber, 2013).

Page 236, 'the act of writing is an act of attempted comprehension…'
Joyce Carol Oates and Meghan O'Rourke, 'Why We Write About Grief',
New York Times, 26 February 2011, <http://www.nytimes.com/2011/02/27/
weekinreview/27grief.html?pagewanted=all> (last accessed 27 October 2014).

INDEX